Investing Tips Grampa Taught Us

A Guide to Financing College Costs and more

Elizabeth Masson and Eric Eber

Authors Choice Press

San Jose New York Lincoln Shanghai

Investing Tips Grampa Taught Us
A Guide to Financing College Costs and More

Authors Choice Press
an imprint of iUniverse.com, Inc.

For information address:
iUniverse.com, Inc.
5220 S 16th, Ste. 200
Lincoln, NE 68512
www.iuniverse.com

Originally published by Financial Press

ISBN: 0-595-17916-9

Printed in the United States of America

Table of Contents

Acknowledgments

Since neither of us is old enough to even qualify as a state-licensed professional, we hope readers of these pages understand the subject matter is presented without any intention of offering accounting, legal or other professional services. It is our recommendation and also that of the publisher: if expert assistance is needed, the services of the appropriate qualified independent professional should be retained.

Elizabeth

All things considered, we must also admit our purpose is not entirely altruistic. One of our long range goals is to produce a respectable amount of sales of this book in order to provide for a generous addition to our college fund as well as for the newborn twins, Matthew and John and our future brothers and sisters.

We want to thank Grandma Betty for her assistance and patience and Eric's dad, my Uncle Steve for his analyses and contributions. Uncle Steve is president of a capital management company in Florida. He was recognized as the fourth best money manager in the United States, in his category, from 1987 through 1993. His columns and commentaries are regularly featured on local television and in the newspapers.

Eric

We are especially grateful to our Grampa, Victor Eber, for his translation of our messages and artful handling of graphics and text. In 1949, Grampa founded the company now owned and managed by Uncle Steve. He taught finance and investing as an adjunct professor at the University of Miami and Florida International University for 41 years. Grampa wrote three books, the last of which was *Up Your Equity — Build Your Personal Net Worth*. and was a feature, syndicated writer for the *Daily Business Review*.

Grampa put his money where his theories were and achieved financial goals even greater than planned. His theories on long-term investments were put to the ultimate test of proven results in the more than four decades of teaching, preaching and practice. By and large, this is what he taught his children and now, hopefully is conveying to his grandkids and other kids and parents who need a road map to guide them through the pitfalls of investing for college and other goals.

We want to thank editor Jennifer Whitehead, attorney Ann Fisher, literary specialists Rosario Lopez Guerrero and John Shaw, journalist James Russell, author Taffy McCallum and publisher Charity Johnson for their assistance.

Thanks to Christine Tripp for her cover illustration and artwork, to Phil Frank for his cartoons and to computer expert Luis Bardi for his technical help.

Our special appreciation goes to project manager Mary Andrews for her talented input and invaluable counsel.

The Twins
Matthew
and John

Preface

Mom tells us Grampa had 155 pages of his book, *Strategies for Investing*, in place in June 1984, when the publisher asked for another chapter with details of **his own** financial plan. Grampa said this was too personal. He would rather talk about the sins of his childhood before disclosing something as personal as his own finances. So, Grampa put his manuscript away.

Strategies for Investing was originally intended as a guide for the specialized needs of professionals for retirement and investment planning. This was to be a sequel to Grampa's first books written in 1969 and 1971, *The Pros and Cons in Financial Management for Professionals* and *Up Your Equity—Build Your Personal Net Worth*.

When my Mom found the unfinished manuscript, she asked Grampa if he'd help us revise, update and finish the book. He agreed, but expected Mom and Uncle Steve

Mom found an old manuscript written by Grampa in 1984.

Elizabeth

to supervise the editing and he would assist as needed, in addition to doing the graphics and text placement.

Grampa still had stories to tell and would talk in long bursts on the honor and glory of saving and investing to guarantee future goals. My folks (and Eric's too) would, as always, flee when Grampa started one of his homilies. Frankly, I enjoyed his stories. Eric always laughed when he talked. I did too.

Grampa's books and more than 150 nationally syndicated articles are unique; they reflect his lifetime of successful planning and investing. But there's more reason for this book than paying homage to our grandfather.

Most writers who deal with retirement are usually more seriously concerned with their own. Their books are often written to accumulate dollars for **their own** personal net worth.

Grampa's books were not written to increase his wealth. He had already become more than well-off through the application of his long-term investing disciplines to business, professional and equity

Grampa tells us how to get rich slowly

Eric

involvements, particularly his dedication to the disciplines for **getting rich slowly.** Grampa was, and still is, primarily a teacher. His 41 years as an adjunct professor at the University of Miami and Florida International University were his way of paying back for the fine education he received on academic scholarships.

As we begin this presentation, my cousin and coauthor Eric has just reached the ripe young age of five (5) months. He is truly proud of his dad (my Uncle Steve) the professional money manager. Uncle Steve manages to save a moderate portion of his earnings as does my Mom, the frugal one, and the kid sister who used to be the real estate specialist of Uncle's capital management company. She "retired" to spend more time with me.

Do you remember the fable of the grasshopper and the ant?

Mom absorbed most of her father's constant litany of Aesop's fables as he translated them to morality lectures on personal economics. Grampa's favorite recitation was the fable of "The Grasshopper and the Ant." Remember it? Subsequently set to a jingle, the grasshopper loafed around all summer dancing to the tune, "The World

Owes Me A Living." Meanwhile, the ant was busy gathering hazelnuts and other fodder and storing them for winter. The other day, when Grampa innocently asked, in the presence of my folks and Eric's if we ever heard the story of the Grasshopper and the Ant, Mom and Uncle hurriedly left the room without saying a word.

Eric and I then decided to share with you, our fellow grandkids, the wisdom, secrets and tips of long-term money management as taught by Grampa.

His definition of investing is a dedication to the disciplines of slowly growing money set aside for investment, the slower the better, the more time available, the better. The more time available, the lower the required growth rate (i.e., rate of return or yield) and, therefore, the smaller degree of required risk. And most important of all, he still insists only a fool would take greater risk than required. Grampa would repeat, over and over again: if we could attain our goals with a lower yield, it would be nonsense to be-

come impatient and seek higher returns (i.e., therefore, assume a greater risk).

A long-term outlook is the fundamental ingredient for his formula for the successful attainment of life goals. A favorite "original" line of Grampa's is:

If you don't know
where you are going,
any road will get you there. *

KISS =
♦ Keep
♦ It
♦ Simple
♦ Smarty

Another of Grampa's caveats, *malapropriated* from an unknown source is **KISS** *(Keep It Simple, Smarty)*. He loved to tell us how Albert Einstein was so easy to read and understand. Grampa was 15, a freshman at the then City College of New York, when he read Einstein's *General Theory of Relativity* and a book of essays by Bertrand Russell. "Einstein's theory was easy to read and understand," Grampa said. "His general theory had only one formula ($E=MC^2$). And not a single chart!"

On the other hand, Bertrand Russell would pontificate and stray. "He had sentences that ran one and a half pages!" Grampa would get red in the face as he

---

* He reluctantly was compelled to confess this line came from Lewis Carroll in his famous classic, *Alice in Wonderland*.

shouted, "It took six hours to read 40 pages and I couldn't understand a thing!"

He loved to remind us about rereading Russell almost 50 years later and still having difficulty understanding his rambling style. Grampa made an early commitment in his multifaceted career as professor, author and founding principal of an investment company to keep it simple: no jargon, fancy words or long sentences.

So, with these caveats in mind, Eric and I intend to write about investing the way it was taught to us by Grampa. We also hope to do this without using "big" words and fancy, technical talk. The editors have promised to review our pages to keep these messages simple and easy to read so that readers will not be intimidated.

Let me remind you. My name is Elizabeth, the senior member of the writing team. Eric, as you already know, is five months as we begin this book in July 1993 and I, twenty-two months old.

CHAPTER 1
Investing Can Be Easy

S ome of us are born with active financial genes like coauthor Eric, who is also fortunate to be happy and analytical. This book should be helpful to all kids, but is mainly directed to those of average intelligence with a desire to establish early plans for funding college education and lifetime goals. It will cover the basics in taking control of investing strategies. We also hope it will serve as a guide to our parents, most of whom are too occupied handling the family's present needs. They are too busy to worry about such things as funding college and other future needs. Too bad! Delegating money to the future has a serious flaw:

Elizabeth's
Mom

> *One loses the opportunities of the built-in magic of compound growth and the blessings of long-term planning with practically no risk. Risk, as measured by volatility, is significantly lowered over the longer term.*

History proves, investing in 15-year or longer periods reduces risk to a minimum. Thus, the long-term investor gains far greater rewards at less risk.

Eric's Mom

As a bonus, this book should also serve as a guide for concerned families to avoid the anxieties of last minute scrambling for college funds due to their failure to plan earlier.

Would you like to know the secret to investing that practically guarantees achieving long-term goals? **It is simplicity**. The more **user-friendly** our investment style, the more confident we can be of making money in the long run.

Sadly, this insight is not easy to adopt because of the many diversions and pitfalls that lead the best of us grandkids astray. There are all kinds of glittering distractions offering quick bucks or fun today. But we don't need quick gains! There's plenty of time—fifteen or more years—and time is the most important ingredient for compounding magic in long-term investing. We can rack up a superb lifetime investment record with just two or three good stock-only, no-load mutual funds. That's basically all we really need to know and more importantly, all we need to sustain the strength of our focus.

Investing is easy if we buy the simple things in accordance with a careful plan. More on this in later chapters. Kids with money to invest for college might also want to learn about the stock market. There are many books and courses on learning how to invest in the stock market.

There are teachers, members of the media, and others who say bad things about wealth: it's the root of all evil and other kinds of negative stuff. But a healthy, positive view about money helps us gain a perspective of balance which pays rich dividends in attaining happy, fruitful and well constructed lives. Charities, and even universities with professors who knock money, seek funds too as do museums and symphonies. There is hardly an artistic group that does not receive financial help via donations. Since we deal with money every day, a positive attitude about it can make our lives pleasant and productive. Those

Dollars properly invested are always working and growing, enabling us to sleep restfully while they "march" day and night.

who underrate dollars and fail to take responsibility for themselves usually regret this in later years. When we learn the value of money, and deal with it in a mature, balanced manner, our lives, and of course the lives of our future families, will be enriched. Planning for the future and living within our earnings while saving and investing is the formula for a rewarding, anxiety-free lifestyle.

If you do not believe any of this, or think of the above as an unacceptable philosophy for your own personal reasons, don't waste time reading any more. Go to the nearest post office and return this book with a request for a refund.

Grampa says having money can be like having our own green soldiers marching twenty-four hours a day to a cadence comfortable to us. Money is useful, and if deployed intelligently, provides many of the good things in life. Grampa likes to say money may not be the most important thing in life, but it sure comes in a close second to whatever is in first place. One of his favorite lines is *"Having money transforms an old-*

ster like me into a distinguished gentleman whose jokes are always funny."

People who consider money as an end in itself, as something they just want to accumulate, aren't likely to manage their green soldiers very well. We are never too young to decide how we feel about money. The fact that we are interested in saving and investing money, rather than just having our parents give it to us, is a good sign. We understand money can be a reflection of our own self-esteem. We believe we can do things that are worthwhile. That's about the same as saying we think **we** are worthwhile! And that's a super feeling!

But money can be used to buy things, and it also can be used to make more money. Let's put aside buying things and providing for our daily living. After all, that's what parents (and grandparents) should do for us. This book's principal purpose is to help ourselves (and our parents) make an early dedication to planning for our college education. We also want to make sure that some money is put aside for emergencies as well as for the future.

A healthy, positive view about money pays dividends in fruitful and well-balanced lives.

If not money, what else is in second place?

Let's focus on making our money grow. Suppose we already have several thousand dollars. Or, we've just inherited a good sum of money and don't know what to do with it. Are banks the best place to keep nest eggs growing for the long-term? We think not. Banks may be better than keeping our money in the cookie jar, but only for payment of current expenses, unplanned repairs to house and car and for a longer term only to maintain a minimum checking account.

Banks pay interest that is too low for long-term investing. The myth about safety was exploded in the early 1990s with the mass of savings and loan bankruptcies and scandals such as the CenTrust Bank and Lincoln National Savings. Some people still prefer bank savings because of federal insurance on their deposits. Unfortunately, there are many who hang on to old and unproductive habits.

Consider some other choices for investment. We could literally put our college funds in other people's businesses. Many big businesses sell shares of stock in their company to the general public. If we buy shares of

Should we invest in

bank CDs or mutual funds?

stock in a company, we get more than a piece of paper. What we are buying is a part of that company. We have become part owners of that business. As part owners (or shareholders) in the company we make money if the company does, but we can also lose if the company is not successful. It is a risk, just like starting any business.

Inheritance?

Buying and selling those shares of stock is big business for stockbrokers. If a lot of people want to buy the stock of a certain company, the price goes up. If people start selling those shares and there aren't many interested in buying them, the price goes down. Sometimes a stock that can be bought for very little will start to go higher and higher because of good and expanding business; the company is going to make a lot of money. If the company does make money, it may share some of it with the people who own stock. This is called paying dividends. Those who invested even modestly in companies like Walmart and Microsoft when they got started could be millionaires today.

Rather than hope we get lucky, we prefer to apply principles of long-term invest-

Prospecting
for
stock
"nuggets"
is a
low
percentage
way
to
get rich.

ing to common applications that will still produce wealth even though more slowly. Slow growth, almost by definition, means lower risk-taking.

The trick is to watch out for today's complex financial marketplace and buy the simple things that we can analyze ourselves. In the world of money, one or two clear and strong ideas can make us richer than we ever believed possible.

We recommend temporarily putting our initial dollars into a money market account with free checking account privileges instead of a bank. Before selecting the vehicle for college investing, let's study up a bit and review the alternatives for long-term investing to grow our college fund.

A few words are in order on other areas of investing. Some people make their money grow by investing in land, lots, houses and other properties.

One of Grampa's favorite puns is:

"You've got to get a lot while you're young."

Although this may be a good way for those who have the patience and ability to manage property, it is not for everybody.

Eric's folks prefer stocks and bonds to real estate. My Mom and Dad like to put money and time into their own house, selling it and reinvesting in another home 5-7 years later. They enjoy improving the house and increasing their living comforts while gradually building significant equity.

It's pleasant to think about buying a vacant lot for $10,000 and in six months selling it for $30,000 to a company that needed land for a new plant. On the other hand, we can pay $10,000 and be forced to hold a lot for more years than we want.

Sometimes we can't get out even by selling at a loss if nobody will buy. Grampa says he has owned property he couldn't even give away because there was no market.

Another of Grampa's favorite stories is about making a lot of money on a parcel of land he couldn't sell even at an enormous loss. Many years later, when a group showed up who wanted the property, he sold it at a big profit.

where should we invest our money?

Those who have done well in real estate investing like to talk about their huge winnings. But few talk about the frustration of paying taxes and maintaining their investment over a period of many years.

It's no fun being locked in, but this is one of the drawbacks of real estate investing. When the market is slow, we may be compelled to hold our property much longer than ever intended. Grampa keeps reiterating:

Grampa tells us real estate is rarely sold; it is bought only when there is a market for it.

"Real estate is not sold; it is bought, and only when there is a market for it."

This can produce mixed results. The good part about being forced to hold property for the longer term is the growth in value that comes with time. This is why some get rich because of "bad luck" in not being able to sell their real estate when they want.

We can invest in many different things besides buildings and land. Some people buy paintings; others buy gold and silver. Some invest in gold, semi-precious stones, diamonds and/or coins, while others buy old books or antiques as investments.

People who buy and sell in a matter of weeks or months are called traders rather than investors. An investor, with special objectives such as college funding or retirement, will hold some objects for years, sometimes many years.

He may buy paintings from an unknown artist for only $50 each and hold them for 20 years until the painter is world famous. The investor sells his $50 paintings for $50,000 each. Or, by that time the painter's work may be judged so bad that the investor can only give it away.

For most of us, art should be acquired for enjoyment rather than as an investment.

A wise investor takes pains to learn all about the books or stones or paintings he's buying—or hires someone who knows about these things. He buys paintings or other art principally for pleasure. For our purposes, art will not be further discussed as an investment option.

There are those who like to invest in mortgages. This is another investment area that requires special knowledge and time available to select and manage.

Our college investment strategy is limited to common stock (equity) investing only. Believe it or not, stock investing has

$1.00 invested in 1925 = $800.08 today!

proven to be as good a method as any to provide for long-term goals such as college funding and usually is the most popular way for passive investing.

Kids and their families with money to invest for college might find it interesting to learn more about the stock market. There are many other books on how to invest for the long-term.

More than a few universities also offer courses in adult education programs on personal investing and financial planning. Most courses deal with investing in stocks, portfolio management and mutual funds.

The popularity of how-to-invest courses is mainly due to the general public's increased concern with saving for college. More people are interested in stocks because investments may be made in small amounts and on a more regular basis than generally required for real estate, mortgages or hard assets.

Also, the knowledge is spreading that stocks do better than twice as good as bonds, CDs and Treasury notes.

Read this again →

Over the past 68 years, stocks have provided the greatest overall increase in wealth by a large margin. An investment in large company stocks, with all income invested, grew at an annual compound rate of 10.3%!

**Source:
1994 Yearbook
(Ibbotson Associates)**

CHAPTER 2
Setting Up Our Plan

To attain our investment goals, we need space on the wall to display all the promotions and sales pitches constantly targeting us. Should we buy this mutual fund or that one? How do we choose among stocks? Why aren't bonds and annuities suitable for young folks? What risks should we take?

There are logical answers to these questions, but only if we start with a good, long-term investment plan. Once we've drawn that plan, the enigma of money becomes clear. We will learn the kinds of investments to consider. More importantly, we learn which to avoid. Getting rich quickly is an illusion, and sadly keeps many of us from ever achieving any of our money goals.

Our planning offers no formulas for getting rich quickly. Instead, we discuss simple plans with strategies to create realistic funds

for our college education. Worthwhile long-term planning is simple and as boring as watching grass grow in the backyard.

Incredible!

MEASURING GOALS

As with any of our goals, we need to know how much money we need and when we will need the fund. In Chapter 8, plans are discussed for our college funding.

PLANNING FOR OTHER FUNDS

Planning for college requires the same application of philosophy and investing as any of our other future money goals. Of course, any change in the time frame obliges appropriate modifications in the investing program. For example:

Whitewater rafting down the Colorado— See the Grand Canyon 8 days— $1500 for all expenses

Cousin Eric is less than six months old. His college plan allows for approximately 16-17 years of accumulation. If Eric also cared to fund a rafting trip down the Colorado River as a gift to himself upon his graduation from high school, there is a simple calculation for the required contribution.

First of all, the trip would cost considerably less than four years of college.

A fund of $1500 to be accumulated by the year 2006 should be enough to pay for this trip.

Assuming an estimated annual compound yield of 10% (i.e., eight percent *capital growth + two percent dividend reinvested.... a conservative estimate*), a monthly contribution of $5.43, beginning on July 1, 1993, will grow to $1500 to be accumulated by the year 2006.

Can you believe 18¢ a day will take care of an all expense trip of eight days rafting down the Colorado River through the magnificent Grand Canyon! Could planning be more simple and doable?

Let's consider this simple solution as the basis for calculating any of our intermediate-to long-term money goals. Let's try another simple problem on our pocket computers.

Eric is ecstatic about the prospects for his rafting trip in the summer of 2006 and painlessly puts aside 18¢ every day. Now he's curious to know how much is needed to accumulate one million dollars ($1 million) by the time he is 45 years old and ready to retire on his sailboat.

So with the help of Grampa's calculator, here's the answer:

A contribution of

→ $3.18 per day, or,

→ $95.41 per month, or

→ $1122.92 per year

will grow to $1,000,000 by 2038 (i.e., 45 years) assuming a monthly contribution to the fund of $95.41 and an average return of 10% (including reinvested dividends).

Let's look at this a bit more thoroughly. This monthly contribution for 45 years adds up to $51,521 (excluding interest). Even more amazing is the smaller amount that could be invested in a single sum.

Can you believe:
A lump sum
contribution of $13,720 on
July 1, 1993, should grow to
$1,000,000
in forty five (45) years!

This is based on the same conservative growth assumption of 10% compounded annually!

Here's another and even more basic illustration of the incredible magic of compound growth:

If offered a choice between A and B, which should we choose?:

**A. $1 million dollars
    on October 31**

or

**B. 1¢ on October 1 which
    will double on October
    2 and again double on
    October 3 and so on
    each day until October
    31 when we receive the
    final computed
    amount?**

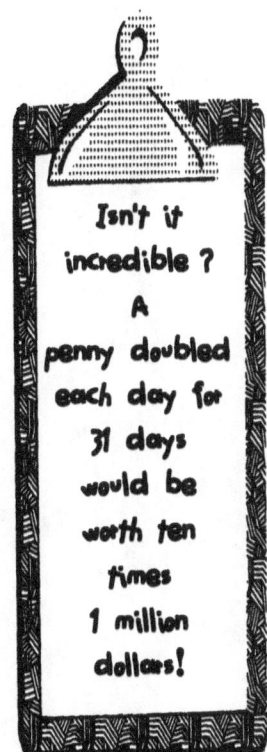

Isn't it
incredible ?
A
penny doubled
each day for
31 days
would be
worth ten
times
1 million
dollars!

You may be surprised to learn that the choice should be for the daily-doubling penny. While compounding rates are usually considerably less than doubling each day, the lesson in the effect of compounding is clearly demonstrated.

Let's see how this looks, day by day, in the following calculation:

Day		Amount
October	1	$ 0.01
October	2	$ 0.02
October	3	$ 0.04
October	4	$ 0.08
October	5	$ 0.16
October	6	$ 0.32
October	7	$ 0.64
October	8	$ 1.28
October	9	$ 2.56
October	10	$ 5.12
October	11	$ 10.24
October	12	$ 20.48
October	13	$ 40.96
October	14	$ 81.92
October	15	$ 163.84
October	16	$ 327.68
October	17	$ 654.36
October	18	$ 1,308.72
October	19	$ 2,617.44
October	20	$ 5,234.88
October	21	$ 10,469.76
October	22	$ 21,939.52
October	23	$ 43,879.04
October	24	$ 87,758.08
October	25	$ 175,516.16
October	26	$ 351,032.32
October	27	$ 702,064.64
October	28	$ 1,404,129.28
October	29	$ 2,808,258.56
October	30	$ 5,616,517.12

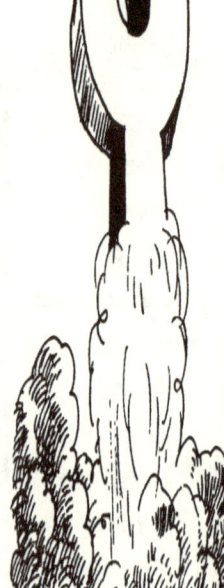

October 31   Total **$ 10,333,034.24**

To summarize this graphic example of the magic of compounding:

- 1¢ doubled each day for 31 days will grow to more than $10 million by the 31st day!

- A single sum contribution in 1993 of $13,720 or monthly contributions of $95.41 at 10% per annum will grow to one million dollars ($1,000,000) by the year 2038.

The magic
of
interest
Compound-
ing
becomes
easier to
understand
because
of
Computers.

Eric and I are amazed by this incredible experience with compounding. Grampa assures us that he has been fascinated with this magic since 1972 when the first hand-held computers became available. Before then, it was necessary to spend hour after hour doing a single problem in compounding interest over a long period of time. There were also tables available for periods up to 30 years with a range of rates. Grampa tells us how he tested his model HP80 for hours at a time, fascinated by the speed with which he could calculate in seconds what literally took hours using rate tables.

Grampa joyously retells the story of the sale of the island of Manhattan in 1626. Using his new HP80 to invest the $24 received by the Algonquin Indians, he calculated how the $24 would grow for 346 years at various annual compound rates.

Read on in Chapter 3 for details.

Chapter 3
Long-Term Investing

Even after reviewing the miracle of growing a million dollars as illustrated in the previous chapter, Eric and I asked Grampa to recheck our figures. We know about the magic of compound interest, but this still is hard to believe. Grampa told us about his now oft-quoted article, originally published in 1972.

It was about Peter Minuit, boss of a traveling unit of the Dutch West India Company. In 1626, he acquired a 22.3 acre parcel of land called Manhattan from the then resident Algonquin Indians for costume jewelry valued at $24. In 1972, Grampa converted this $24 via the magic of compounding with his first hand-held computer to the then value of more than $72 billion! He jokingly concluded the Indians had overcharged the Dutch since the total assessed value of New York City (*the*

$24. invested at 6% in 1626 would be worth $259 billion in 1994

other four boroughs in addition to the original island Manhattan), was calculated in 1972 to be worth $72 billion!

In 1626, Peter Minuit of the Dutch West India Company paid $24 in costume jewelry to the Algonquin Indians for Manhattan's 22 acres.
(Photograph from World Book Encyclopedia)

Editor's Note:

Just to bring us up-to-date to 1994:

An additional 22 years of annual compounding at 6% (1972 to 1994), takes the $72 billion accumulated tax-assessed value of the City of New York to the astronomical value of more than $259 billion. The incredible magic of compound interest!

How can things be so simple? The expression we have been taught over and over: *"If it sounds too good to be true, it must be too good to be true"* makes us again wonder, "What's the catch?"

One might assume the catch could be in the assumed rate of interest. This is not it. The problem in achieving a long-term accumulating investment would be in dealing with the uncertainties of life that we all must endure, if not predict, anticipate or control, ranging from the need to replace tires or the car itself to the more serious problems in dealing with long-term sickness, injury, disability or death of a family member. The second, a corollary to the first, is adhering to the discipline of not tampering with or borrowing from the fund. This may be hard to do without insurance or other provisions to provide for emergencies.

The compounding concept will produce its magic so long as we do our part in securing guarantees from "The Higher Authority" to protect us from misfortunes against which we cannot prepare. The subject of insurance is not covered in this book, but serious insurance planning is a must in order to provide a safety net. This should include consideration of disability, major health, accident and liability coverage as a first priority after which attention should be directed to coverage for home, automobiles and other big-ticket items.

The subject of insurance is not covered in this book!

Those who want excitement in their investing programs might better consider short-term ventures such as betting at horse and dog tracks.

Long-term programs can be as exciting as watching grass grow. Grampa likes to say there's no reason why long-term planners can't also go to the track or indulge in other games for the quick turnover of money. But, he says, only after our serious planning is in place.

In fact, Grampa insists fun and games with extra dollars can be more enjoyable **after** one has set aside serious money in a long-term program. Can you imagine how much more we would enjoy boating trips, skiing and exotic vacations when there is no anxiety or guilt because we have not provided for our serious lifetime planning?

Long-term planning is boring but once in place, we can enjoy short-term pleasures!

Considerations for
long-term stock investing

1. **Stocks with low risk** have outper-formed bonds, Treasury notes and CDs (2 to 1) since 1925.

2. **Keep it simple.** Blue chip stocks are all you should consider. Options or futures, com-modities, and limited partnerships are not for young grandkids. As few as 12 stocks may serve as a portfolio to provide the required diversification to minimize risk. **Be careful:** selecting stocks individually can be a fun game, but usually only professionals or seri-ous amateurs have the time and acquired skills necessary for success.

3. **Best bet:** If we are not ready to follow our recommended preference for an inde-pendent money manager, it's better to choose the mutual fund (stocks only) route and avoid individual stock picking. No-load mutual funds provide full-time profes-sional money management, which we nor-mally cannot do for ourselves. Managers diversify investments and balance our risks. Diversification can be further in-

creased by selecting several no-load mutual funds. (See details in Chapter 7.)

4. Hold mutual funds for the long-term.

5. Put a fixed sum of money into mutual funds at regular intervals—at least once a year, if not monthly. Monthly installments are best for several reasons:

- ♦ adds to compounding "magic"

- ♦ increases cost-averaging benefit.

Don't worry about "bad" markets which usually provide good buying opportunities for long-term investors because prices are so low. History has proven:

whether for 10, 20, or 25 years, it's better to stay fully invested all of the time.

6. Do not withdraw dividends.
Reinvestment of dividends over a longer period produces even more magic.

Kids and families should remember:

✔ Over long periods of time, stocks have out-performed inflation by roughly seven percent (7%) annually. That's a better average real return than you'll get from other financial investments.

✔ Over the past 68 years, stocks have provided the greatest overall increase in wealth by considerable margins. An investment in large company stocks (with all income reinvested) grew at an average annual rate of 10.3% — more than twice the annual return on bonds!

very important!

CHAPTER 4
WHERE TO INVEST:
REAL ESTATE, STOCKS
AND OTHER ASSETS

Grown-ups sometimes consider other options for a balanced investment plan. For the present, this discussion will be short since our primary purpose is to understand and work with the principles of long-term investing by limiting our main focus to stock investing only. A more complete study of real estate, bonds, money market instruments, annuities and other real assets as investment alternatives will require a separate book or two.

Therefore, the summary discussion in this chapter will be restricted to the more accessible interests in real estate partnerships and syndicated forms, all of which

For now, we're only going to concentrate on stock investing

provide management. While real estate is still one of Grampa's favorite vehicles for long-term investment, he warns us this is not for everybody, especially us grandkids. It requires special training and education.

Therefore, we limit our quick discussion to real estate that can be acquired with management included. This is available by buying interest or shares in limited partnerships, investment trusts or syndications. Diversified programs are offered by stock brokerage houses, insurance companies and even commercial banks.

Kids should not invest in real estate without qualified, professional advice.

Most real estate limited partnerships and other so called tax shelter limited partnerships are complicated and require a thorough review of the offering prospectus by an **independent** professional, such as your family's accountant or tax lawyer.

In recent years, Grampa warns, there has been an increase in the number of "professionals" who participate in the selling process by earning commissions. According to Grampa, this eliminates them from independent status.

The public syndication business, promoted by major selling organizations, includes properties other than real estate. Most, whether oil, gas, heavy equipment, etc., are promoted strictly as tax shelters with tempting write-offs. These will not be separately discussed in this section. It's so important for us to obtain our own independent review and validation.

The reason for the rise of the public syndication business is simple. Public syndications offer us the opportunity to participate in managed real estate programs at relatively low unit costs. The syndicator is the general partner who buys the property, manages it, and while collecting assorted fees along the way, eventually takes a percentage of the sales proceeds. Too often even our trusted independent reviewer knows little, if anything, about the economic and other values of the syndicated assets.

Grampa also points out the disadvantages of real estate investing. Sometimes we are locked into the investment for longer periods than we like. This lack of liquidity is a type of risk that is unacceptable for many of us planning to fund our college costs. Tuition cannot be paid with

watch out for the "too-good-to-be-true deals!

real estate units! If, when college enrollment time comes, the real estate assets are
not saleable, it could put a serious crimp
in our college plans. This lack of liquidity
removes real estate ownership from consideration in our present planning.

However, there are offerings that minimize risk and offer liquidity via trading on
public stock exchanges. Some real estate
investment trusts (REITs) may offer the
fixed return of government insured mortgages plus participation in their appreciation. These participations can be made in
denominations of $1,000 or more, and can
be attractive additions to our investment
portfolios. Grampa tells us REITs, when included in a balanced stock portfolio, have
recently come back into favor, offering the
best of all worlds of real estate investment
with the added advantages of risk minimi-
zation and liquidity.

A major factor in the attractiveness of
real estate as an investment vehicle is the
public's general perception of real estate
as an inflation hedge. In periods of hyper-
inflation, capital is directed to real estate
with the expectation that values will rise

JUST HOW

MUCH

LIQUIDITY

IS NEEDED?

higher than the rate of inflation. This was true in the 1970s. However, currently the rate of inflation has dropped from high double digits to less than 4% in 1994, and the rates of return on real estate has also dropped.

Presently, in this period of sustained disinflation, which Grampa says should remain in manageable single digit levels for at least the next few years, it remains to be seen whether real estate investments will outperform equities. This may depend more on individual selection of properties purchased and expertise of the venture's general partners.

Which is the greater inflation hedge? Real estate? Or stocks?

Would you believe, the answer is both! Especially if the acquisitions are timely! Real estate purchased at favorable prices before a period of rapid appreciation (i.e., an inflationary cycle) is an inflation hedge. However, real estate purchased at the top of a cycle, such as in 1981, when prices were peaking and the inflationary trend was reversing, could well turn out to be anything but an inflation hedge.

The same can be true with stocks. If we are truly in a sustained period of disinflation, lower interest rates, increased corporate growth and reduced unemployment, stocks could well be the inflation hedge for years to come.

Grampa repeats, "The answer is, of course, both real estate and stocks can be inflation hedges, if timely purchased."

The opposite is true if long-term investment additions to portfolios are made in either vehicle at too high prices. The speculative excesses in real estate rose and fell in the 1970s. In 1974, there was a bust.

A lot of real estate had been sold with negative cash flow based on unrealistic expectations of future growth. The market fell apart with disastrous results for REITs, some of which still have not recovered. But when the inflation spiral rose again, there was a speculative fever which resulted in extraordinary gains for a few years. In 1979, it was not uncommon for real estate speculators to buy a house for $100,000 and sell it six months later for $150,000.

On the other hand, money and debt instruments such as CDs, Treasury bills, regular savings accounts, bonds and annuities are hardly ever considered inflation hedges. This is another reason Grampa teaches us kids to avoid these in our long-term investing strategies.

Real estate, like stock, is not an inflation hedge if last year's fashions are bought at current year's high prices.

OTHER INVESTMENTS

PRECIOUS METALS AND ART

Grampa thinks gold is too risky!!

Inflationary cycles also attract investors to gold, diamonds, art and other assets that usually increase in value at a rate greater than inflation. These assets are favored also because they are not subject to taxes while they increase in value as is real estate. Presently gold is still a valuable commodity that serves some as a store of value, a hedge against inflation and a substitute for depreciating paper currencies. Gold can be owned in many forms: jewelry, coins, bullion and stock in gold mining companies. Although gold jewelry goes up in value as the price of gold rises, this is not the most effective way to invest in gold, unless jewelry is fashioned out of gold coins. Gold coins can be purchased purely for their gold content or numismatic value. For example, South African Krugerrands are sold for gold content rather than numismatic value, whereas the U.S. double-eagle ($20) has greater numis-

matic value. Other coins with varying combinations of collector and gold value are:
Mexican 50 peso, Austrian ducats and corona, Hungarian Korona and English sovereigns.

Since 1975, U.S. citizens can legally
buy gold bullion. Gold, in whatever form,
is a risky investment. This can be determined by its price volatility. From 1975 to
1980, the price of gold rose from $175 to
$800 for an annual compound rate of 22%.
However, from the $800 price in 1980 to
the $385 price at year end 1983,* the annual rate of decrease was 17.8%. This is
true of the other precious metals such as
silver and platinum and more so in the case
of diamonds and precious stones.

Because of the high risk factor, precious metals, stones and art are not considered investment portfolio vehicles for
the purpose of our discussion of long-term
investing.

At
least
Gold
Makes
Nice
Jewelry!

* As at December 31, 1993,
the price of gold was $394.20
per ounce.

For More Information

YOUR INVESTMENTS
by
L. Barnes
Prentice Hall
Englewood Cliffs, New Jersey

PROTECT YOURSELF
IN REAL ESTATE
by
Robert Irwin
McGraw Hill
New York, New York

MAKING THE MOST
OF YOUR MONEY
by
Jane Bryant Quinn
Simon & Schuster
New York, New York

Questions for Our Parents and Other Advisors

QUESTION 1

How do we determine if our financial advisor is receiving fees or commissions from the seller?

QUESTION 2

Is it legal and ethical to charge a commission in addition to a fee?

QUESTION 3

Is an investment in real estate protection against inflation?

QUESTION 4

What about gold and other commodities for investment purposes? Explain.

QUESTION 5

Do bond investments protect against inflation?

This discussion is designed for kids, and their families, who are serious about as a basic primer for appropriate decision making, selection and management of long-term investment portfolios. Even in this simplified discussion, it is sometimes necessary to use some of the fancy terms and jargon used by portfolio managing professionals.

There is one common goal to all types of investment, whether short or long-term, conservative, aggressive or speculative. This common goal is to achieve maximum rewards for investments at minimum risk. Our goal is to keep this discussion as simple as possible.

There are many scholarly books written analyzing investing rewards and risk. These will be helpful later when we require more sophisticated and specific information.

For the present, our purpose is to prepare our parents and ourselves to initiate basic long-term investing programs as soon as possible.

CHAPTER 5
Understanding Risk

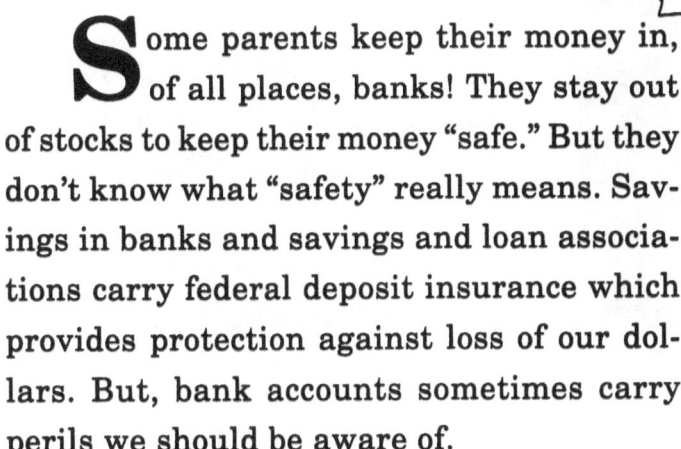

S ome parents keep their money in, of all places, banks! They stay out of stocks to keep their money "safe." But they don't know what "safety" really means. Savings in banks and savings and loan associations carry federal deposit insurance which provides protection against loss of our dollars. But, bank accounts sometimes carry perils we should be aware of.

what is safe?

Bonds and fixed income investments can eat up our future just as surely as if it were tossed into the garbage can. Later on, we will show a table that traces growth of stocks versus bonds, Treasury notes and bills over a 68 year period, relating each period to the rate of inflation. We need to understand the different risks in order to make good investment decisions.

- **Market risk**—the risk of losing money in a bad investment.

This can be managed by:

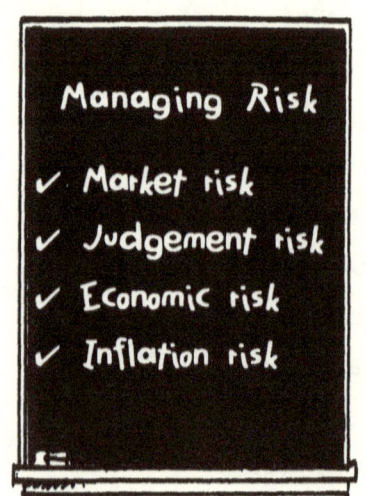

1) Diversifying investments, so that a single loss (even though temporary) doesn't seriously diminish net worth

2) Buying only the boring stuff—such as no-load mutual funds (see Chapter 7)

3) Skipping the trendy propositions of stockbrokers and "market-timers"

- **Bad judgment risk**—the risk of losing money due to hasty research, panicking in volatile markets or deviating from set plans

- **Economic risk**—the jolt your portfolio takes when the economy drops. This risk is handled by avoiding speculative investments that are vulnerable to re-

cessions: limited partnerships in real estate or oil, cattle, etc. whose units are
difficult, if not impossible, to sell

- **Inflation risk**—the risk of losing the
  purchasing power of capital. Presently
  dormant, inflation is the threat to fixed-
  income investors. After inflation and
  taxes, money instruments including
  bonds, certificates of deposit or Treasuries yield almost nothing. Your money
  doesn't really grow; its purchasing
  power decreases.

GRRRRRRR...RRRRIIIIP!!

This can be handled by:

Stocks help "stretch" the dollar in periods of inflation!

1) Limiting permanent sums of cash in
   money market mutual funds and
   similar short-term investments

2) Avoiding bonds

3) Putting most of your money into
   stocks for real growth

Grampa likes to remind us: from the beginning of time people have striven for four things:

- ✔ Food and shelter
- ✔ Love
- ✔ Security
- ✔ A risk-free, growth portfolio

Here's how well (or how poorly) all the popular investments survive inflation:

Let's do it with little or no risk!

AVERAGE COMPOUND RETURNS
1926-1989

AFTER INFLATION

U.S. Treasury bills:	0.5 %
Long-term government bonds:	1.4 %
Intermediate-term U.S. bonds:	1.8 %
Common stocks:	7 %
Small-company stocks:	8.9 %

(Inflation for the period, 3.1%.)

Dividends reinvested but not adjusted for income taxes.

Source: Ibbotson Associates, Chicago

The continuity of long-term common stock yields over inflation is not surprising. From 1926 to 1989, stockholders earned 6.65 percent annually after inflation. (The result for the 1926-89 period is different from Ibbotson's, above, because of a slight difference in the measurement approach of several professors from New York University who made their own study.) From 1871 to 1925, stockholders earned 6.63 percent—almost exactly the same. Therefore, it's wise to ignore the short-run market rides however bumpy and wild.

Because history is the only standard we have for forecasting, we can bet that 15 years from now (time for college), common stocks should produce more than a six percent real return over inflation. Since we cannot avoid all risk, we must remember to assume only that amount of risk to support the rate of growth required to accumulate our targeted fund. We'll say this again and again and then one more time:

> It is foolhardy to accept a higher degree of risk than necessary to produce the same dollar goals.

To summarize:

Long-term growth (10-15 years) is best accomplished by making most investments in stocks. Real estate may be an option if we have the skills, patience and access to family adults ready to help bail us out should liquidity be a problem when it's time to pay for college tuition.

We should take the time to put our own plan in writing, even if its brief. Let's review our plan once a year. As Grampa puts it, **"take an annual *fiscal* "** just as he takes an annual *physical* examination with his doctor. If things change, so will our numbers. Grampa likes to joke he has closets filled with plans that have rarely seen daylight. But they are more valuable, he likes to say, than the fancy leather-bound plans issued in even fancier covers by some financial planners. A written plan helps keep us focused and pointing in the direction intended. And, as grampa keeps repeating:

If we don't know where we're going, any road will get us there.

(For more on risk, see Chapter 9.)

CHAPTER 6
Doing It Ourselves
(with a little outside help)

I t's not hard to be our own guru. We need only to know and list our objectives, a few simple financial products and realistic investment expectations. Because we're all relatively young kids, we have time for our investments to mature. We don't need fancy propositions, and since we are too young to be greedy and have already learned not to accept any more risk than we need, we can and will say **"NO!"** to make-money-quick deals. Occasionally, we may need assurance or an expert opinion or two. That's why we have grandparents. In our case, Grampa knows who to call if he doesn't have the answer himself. Be careful of other people's referrals! (See checklist below for checking out referrals).

Just

say

NO!

Stockbrokers and other commission earners should not be considered independent investment advisors.

If we are not comfortable making investment decisions, consider carefully selecting an independent investment advisor. Never mistake a stockbroker for an independent advisor. By definition, a commission-earning salesperson does not qualify as independent, despite any claims to the contrary. Remember, an independent professional only earns fees for services rendered on a per diem (or hourly) basis without any ties or affiliations to the product(s) he or she may recommend. Also beware of those persons who are professionals but working for companies whose income is principally derived from product sales.

Grampa recommends staying away from the commission folks who have something to sell in addition to services. He used to be a certified public accountant (CPA) so he can advise as to tax considerations of our windfall. Start-up advice for handling investment planning should begin with the family CPA.

Just be sure he isn't also a product-selling financial planner.

In addition to answering tax questions, a CPA may also offer general advice, but few are qualified to offer specific investment counsel. Typically, here are the true **independent professionals**:

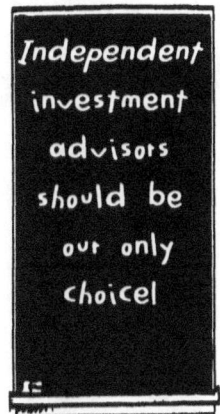

Independent investment advisors should be our only choice!

CERTIFIED PUBLIC ACCOUNTANT (CPA) for tax planning, budget planning, small-business advice and long-term income and savings projections.

Some CPAs have expanded practice as Personal Financial Specialists (PFS). The PFS requires three more years experience plus a tough exam. CPA/PFSs usually charge a fee for service only.

TAX ATTORNEY for complex wills and estate planning.

INDEPENDENT MONEY MANAGER buys, sells and manages on a fee-for-service basis only with no contacts or any rewards from the product companies. CDA/Cadence is a company that provides performance measurement on investment advisors. For information, call 800-833-1394.

Choosing a Financial Planner

watch out for sales pitches!

Seek only independent fee-for-service professionals!

In almost all states, anyone can hold himself or herself out as a financial planner. No tests or licensing is required. Fee-only planners sell no products and are not affiliated with product-selling companies. They only give advice. Fees charged for tax and investment advice can be written off on your income tax returns.

Be wary of "financial planners" employed by banks and stock brokerage houses. Generally speaking, they design plans around company-sold products: certificates of deposit, money-market deposit accounts, stocks and bonds, "loaded" mutual funds and other commission investments.

"The plan" is the reference work that financial planners love to tout. It is usually a thick, loose-leaf binder with a fancy cover that tells us how to behave from cradle to grave. Such plans were the gimmicks of the 1980s. They still are "the bait" for sales of products such as insurance and limited partnerships.

No such plan usually survives any change in the tax laws. We all need a very general plan, outlining financial objectives and investment strategy.

These "planners" may also collect commissions from insurance companies when they sell annuities. Most are decent people, some even community leaders. But as commission-earners, their claim to being independent professionals is tainted.

In order for planners to earn their living, we must buy their product. There are many sad stories of unsound limited-partnerships sold to senior citizens. The simple truth is stockbrokers, insurance sales people and financial planners who earn their livelihood through commissions on product sales **cannot** also wear the hat of an independent professional.

Nevertheless, financial planners who sell products can perform a valuable service to those only seeking to buy their product, whether it be an insurance policy or 100 shares of Merck stock.

Most independent money managers can supply names of experienced and qualified

Beware of self-styled "independent professionals" who earn commissions from product sales.

product sales people who are happy to serve without offering "independent" advice.

A quality planner should have a written summary of his or her credentials and be registered as an investment advisor with the Securities and Exchange Commission (SEC).

Ask for the SEC Form ADV, which discloses education, business background, fees and investment methods. Also, check the planner's CRD form to see if there's a disciplinary history.

The American Institute of Certified Public Accountants offers an APFS tag for Accredited Personal Financial Specialist. A number of colleges and universities also give financial-planning degrees.

These diplomas authenticate the planners as having passed a number of exams areas in such things as taxes, insurance, investments and estate planning. Here are some more tips:

Here are some Questions to ask potential advisors!

- Ask for the names of other clients you can talk to, who have been with the planner for at least a couple of years.

- Ask the planner for a written schedule disclosing all forms of his or her compensation and details of hourly fees. It is also worthwhile to ask what constitutes the income sources for the planner's firm.

- If an outsider makes a referral, ask:

  ➥ Why was this person chosen?

  ➥ What are his or her credentials?

  ➥ Does he or she receive referral fees or other forms of compensation?

- Check with national and local sources for names of planners. Here are some:

  a. The National Association of Personal Financial Advisors. (NAPFA) *They are all fee-only planners. Call 800-366-2732.*

  b. The American Institute of Certified Public Accountants (AICPA Personal Financial Planning Division, 1211 Avenue of the Americas, New York, NY 10036) will give you the names of local CPAs who have taken the courses needed for the Accredited Personal Financial Specialist designation. *CPAs with the personal financial specialist designation <u>do</u> <u>not</u> <u>charge</u> <u>commissions</u> <u>on</u> <u>products</u>. Call 800-862-4272.*

And, least desirable,

c. The Institute of Certified Financial Planners *(7600 E. Eastman Ave. Suite 301; Denver, Colorado; 800-282-7526)*
<u>These</u> <u>planners</u> <u>usually</u> <u>charge</u> <u>sales</u> <u>commissions.</u>

Appearing to be professionals offering "free" advice, some call themselves **financial consultants,** and others employ the term **financial professionals**. Grampa wrote about this subject in his first book. Published in 1971, it was titled, ***The Pros and Cons in Financial Management for Professionals and Executives.***

His book was dedicated to distinguishing the **pros (professionals)** from the **cons (con men)** in offering fee for service financial planning to the public.

In 1993, some major life insurance companies, including Metropolitan, Prudential and New York Life were brought to

the mat by authorities of numerous states
for fraudulent dealings. Some of these
firms were accused of misrepresenting
themselves and their product to special
targeted groups who believed they were
investing in retirement plans. In fact they
were buying the companies products including annuities and limited partnerships
in real estate which carried heavy front
end commissions.

So far, the fines and penalties imposed
have been huge. In late June and July
1994, the major newspapers featured stories about the $102.9 million in additional
fines and refunds the Metropolitan Life Insurance Co. has agreed to pay this year to
more than 40 states. Florida's investiga-
tive report found that Met Life, the
nation's second largest insurer, misled prospective customers throughout the country by touting life insurance as a retirement or savings plan.

watch
out for
the
frauds!

Among the numerous articles which appeared nationally describing the Metropolitan Insurance Company's fraudulent sales
tactics are those which appeared in
Newsweek, January 24, 1994; *Business Week*,

January 17; the *Wall Street Journal*, March 8, 1994; and the *New York Times*, March 9, 1994.

The nation's second largest insurer misled prospective customers throughout the country by touting life insurance as a retirement or savings plan.

Other companies receiving scathing attention include the New York Life Insurance Company which was held liable in a costly case of fraud (*Wall Street Journal*, January 21, 1994) and the Prudential Insurance Company of America which had to take responsibility for their Prudential Securities division's improprieties, including pressuring their brokers as well as brokers who are not properly licensed to sell mutual funds (articles in the *New York Times*, March 3, 1994; the *Wall Street Journal*, March 2, 1994; and *Fortune* magazine, March 21, 1994.)

Despite this current trend exposing premier life insurance and brokerage companies for overly aggressive marketing and fraud, other companies continue to seek greater shares of the marketplace by wearing conflicting hats and offering self-proclaimed professional services.

In 1994, Fidelity Funds, one of the largest and once one of the most prestigious mutual fund companies, again reversed its course and now offers no-load funds sold exclusively through outside brokers. (See Chapter 9).

The summer of 1994 got even hotter than usual. In June, July and August, scathing lead articles dominated the front pages as well as the business sections of most metropolitan newspapers. The *Wall Street Journal* and the *New York Times* led the litany of criticism. They listed prominent institutional sellers such as the Prudential Insurance Company. of America making the change to marketing no-load mutual funds.

It is highly unusual for a brokerage and insurance company to make direct sales to investors without commission especially since Prudential has its own family of approximately 120 funds that provide commissions to its hordes of stockbrokers and insurance agents. There are ever increasing complaints by those in the industry questioning the prioritization for increasing sales over the quality of portfolio management.

This was evident in June 1994 when the New York Stock Exchange censured Merrill Lynch & Company for converting securities of certain customers into common stock without customer permission.

1994 was a long, hot summer in more ways than just climate. A series of articles exposing misrepresentation by some of the largest life insurance and brokerage companies appeared in the wall Street Journal, New York Times and Fortune Magazine

In July 1994, another large brokerage
company, PaineWebber, announced it
would inject an additional $33 million of
its own funds into the firm's flagship
Short-Term U.S. Government Income Fund
to repay investors for losses in risky derivative investments.

And so it seems the saga continues. To
cap it all, even Grampa's favorite, the Vanguard Group, has entered the competition
by aggressively maneuvering for increased
market share by creating a new fund in the
summer of 1994, the Vanguard Tax Managed Fund, with options for:

✔ Growth & Income

✔ Capital Appreciation

✔ Balanced Portfolio

In addition to increasing sales, the ap-
parent game plan is to be the equivalent of
index funds in each category while still producing the benefits of its low management
costs. Additionally, capital gains taxes would
be lowered because of the implied lower
amount of trading in each sector.

Does the addition of new funds make life easier for the small investor? Are they more helpful?

Grampa repeats, while these activities are not illegal, they certainly raise doubts as to whether they are in the best interests of investors.

Our main purpose is not to say nasty things about the prestigious companies discussed. Rather it is to point out the weaknesses of current trends focusing on beat-the-competition marketing which makes it even more important for investors to select truly independent, professional advisors rather than the giant product marketers.

It is important to balance the benefits of the marketing expertise and economies of scale afforded by large product selling companies with the protection of independent professional advisers.

Checks and balances are the core of government. It is equally important for investors to enjoy the benefits of the marketing expertise and economies of scale afforded by these large companies. But for advice and protection from the risk of selling excesses, in addition to balanced, individualized advice, the innocent investor deserves the protection of a professional advisor who is truly independent of any product sales company. The product selling company cannot properly wear the "other hat" of an independent, professional advisor.

For more on this subject, see Chapter 9.

CHAPTER 7
Mutual Fund Investing

No-load mutual funds are best for kids who cannot afford personal money managers.

Kids who can't afford independent money managers like Eric's dad should invest in mutual funds to achieve financial goals including college education. Mutual funds became popular in the mid 1970s, in large measure due to inflation. Investors were frightened and needed to earn more than the five percent offered by savings passbook accounts. This was so because the rate of inflation started producing a loss of spendable funds. The alternative, money market funds, paid a much higher rate of interest. Money market funds were offered by mutual fund companies that invested in short-term interest bearing instruments. Now, most of us kids have some savings in mutual funds.

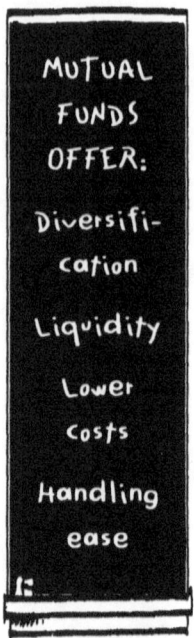

MUTUAL
FUNDS
OFFER:

Diversifi-
cation

Liquidity

Lower
Costs

Handling
ease

Mutual funds, while owned by the investors in the fund, have professional managers who watch over operations and invest on behalf of their shareholders in groups of stocks, bonds or other financial investments called portfolios. A mutual fund share grants holders a proportionate piece of the portfolio, as well as dividends or interest payments and any gains when investments in the portfolio are sold at a profit. It is as if we actually own the stocks ourselves but have someone else manage our portfolio. OK, Eric asks, "Why not buy the individual stocks instead of buying a mutual fund?" Grampa gives several good reasons.

Wouldn't it be better if we could buy more than one share of stock with a small amount of money? If we had $100 to invest, we could buy 10 shares of a stock selling for $10 a share. All our eggs (i.e., $100) would be in one basket. Instead, if we invest the same $100 in shares of a mutual fund, we are buying a piece of many individual companies (i.e., a portfolio). This is called diversification and is an important means of spreading our risk.

If one or two of the companies in the portfolio come upon hard times, it is not going to seriously hurt the fund's value. Diversification is a protection against losses in single companies, and is probably the most important reason for owning shares in a mutual fund.

A second major advantage of mutual funds is the liquidity they offer. With mutual funds, we can sell all or only part of our stocks, and place the money received in a money market account or another mutual fund. It only takes a phone call. There is no transfer of stock certificates or checks. This is called liquidity.

Mutual funds automatically reinvest our dividends no matter how small. It would be difficult and uneconomical, for example, to buy more shares in the one stock we own when a dividend is received.

Mutual Funds offer Liquidity

Finally, Grampa says, although we are smart kids, it takes a lot of time and special education to identify individual stocks that will make for good long-term investments. Even if we have the talent and the time to select good portfolios, keeping track of dividends and business news affecting our individual companies and portfolio changes requires additional expertise and training.

With a mutual fund, management is handled by specially trained personnel. Professional management and efficient record keeping, provided at a very low cost, is probably another good reason Grampa says to invest in mutual funds.

"So," Eric asks, "Why don't all of us kids invest in mutual funds?" One reason for avoiding stocks and mutual funds is fear of what the market calls risk.

Risk refers to the up-and-down activity in the markets and in individual issues. This is called volatility and can be caused by any number of factors such as interest rate changes, inflation or general economic reasons. It is this change, uncertainty and potential for loss that concerns investors. They are afraid of the possibility a company they invest in will come upon hard times causing the stock price to fall.

On the other hand, it is this risk in individual stocks that usually results in higher long-term returns than one gets from CDs or passbook savings. So, the

Mutual Funds offer ease of handling and convenience

measure of volatility (i.e., risk) has as its good side the expectation of greater earnings. The most basic risk we face when investing in common stocks or bonds is any individual company we invest in could have financial difficulties.

There is always the risk our investment in a single company could be lost. The fear of losing our money may be our single greatest obstacle to investing in something other than savings accounts or CDs.

Diversification is the most direct way to manage the risk of setback with a single company. Simply stated, our money is invested in a number of companies instead of just one or two. This is the method professionals use in managing individual portfolios.

Mutual Funds offer a simple way to spread risk via diversification.

Over the past 68 years, the stock market, as measured by the Dow Jones Industrial Average, has achieved an average annual rate of return of slightly more than ten per cent. Grampa insists we should attain this average annual return without incurring an unreasonable amount of risk **(See Chapter 8)**.

Even for those of us who cannot afford an independent money manager like Uncle Steve, mutual funds are the best vehicle to offer independent management. What makes the stock market different from money markets or CDs is the possibility that over short periods of time we really can lose principle value in stocks and bonds, while money markets and CDs do not lose principle. The problem is **these "safer" investments usually offer significantly lower returns over the long-term.**

In fact, over the past 50 years their returns have barely kept up with inflation, while equity investments and common stocks have provided a return five or six percent above the inflation rate. We get what we pay for and we get paid a higher return only when we are willing to accept more risk (volatility).

Mutual funds help beginning investors to diversify their smaller initial investments over a number of stocks. Investing in a mutual fund creates instant diversification of our investment dollars, however small, across a variety of companies and industries. Mutual funds use our money to select a portfolio usually consisting of 30 or more issues. The fund manager does the investment selection for us resulting in instant diversification with the first dollar invested. One company can be having a bad time while at the same time other companies in that fund might be experiencing good fortune resulting in the overall portfolio performing well. That is what diversification is all about.

With $100,000 or more to invest, we could construct our own suitable portfolios. But as we have suggested, identifying single stocks is not easy and takes time and hard work. Professional independent investment management offers the best of all worlds to those who can afford stock selection and flexibility of portfolio management, custom-fitted to individual needs. Grampa taught us that a primary objective of successful investors is to produce consistent long-term returns without long-term losses.

Holding CDs and money market funds over the long-term can prove to be dangerous to our financial health!

The purpose of investing in a mutual fund is to use it to build our wealth over

Leave the driving to the pros.

many years. There are several steps we can take to find and identify the mutual funds right for us in meeting our long-term investment objectives.

Grampa's first recommendation is to buy **no-load** funds directly from the companies without dealing with sales people from stock brokerage firms. Sales commissions, paid to brokers, are called **loads**. When buying funds direct, we have the advantage of putting all of our investment dollars to work for ourselves. There are no commissions! Grampa says no-load mutual funds are usually as good as the ones that are hawked by stock brokers. Our needs are served just as well without paying unnecessary commissions (loads).

The Mutual Fund Educational Alliance (MFEA) at 1900 Erie St., Kansas City, Missouri 64116-3465 is an association sponsored by more than 30 of the better-known mutual-fund organizations. The MFEA offers fine educational materials to the public at modest fees:

✔ **Directing Our Own
Mutual Fund Investments**

✔ **The Investor's Guide to
Low-Cost Mutual Funds**
*Semiannual report on 650 no-load and low-
load mutual funds which can be purchased
without brokers*

The next step is to decide what kinds
of funds, and what fund categories are
right for us. As young kids, we have the
best of all worlds in the length of our time
horizon. This gives us the splendid advantage of additional years to acquire funds.
For example, in our situation Eric is six
months and I am two years old which allows each of us about 15 -17 years time,
respectively, to accumulate our college
funds.

Categories of mutual fund investments listed according to degree of risk are:

- aggressive growth funds
- growth funds
- growth and income funds
- income funds
- money market funds

Grampa says; "Aggressive" no-load funds are not worth the increased risk.

Aggressive growth funds fluctuate in value (i.e., the most volatile **greater risk**) while money market funds have a fixed value.

There are more than 4,000 mutual funds available. These funds range from the conservative, focusing on preservation of capital and source of income, to the most aggressive (speculative), specializing in new companies offering prospects for high growth with plenty of volatility (risk). Because we are young and have more time to accumulate our college money, we can effectively choose within the category of moderate growth funds (i.e., at a lower required rate and, of course, lower risk) to save for college.

Remember: If we can achieve our college goal at the lesser required return (i.e., 10%), why take the greater risk in seeking a higher return?

There are advisory services and newsletters that compare mutual funds according to risk/yield categories. Grampa advises we use those services that stress **long-term performance records.** His favorites are a new service called **Morningstar** (Chicago, Illinois), and **Value Line Mutual Fund Survey** (New York, NY). These services list descriptive materials on long-term performance records of all funds without making recommendations, and are probably the most professional, detailed and complete compilations available. Plastic overlays help us compare results of a ten year investment in each large fund with the Standard and Poor's 500 Index.

Before investing in any mutual fund, we need to have our parents or grandparents review either Value Line Mutual Fund Survey or Morningstar. The alternative is to examine the individual fund's prospectus. **(Few can understand the fine print and boiler plate).** Direct marketed

This is very, very important for us as the #1 rule in our investing!

funds always send a prospectus when information is requested about a fund. A prospectus is almost like a contract: it tells who is responsible for managing the fund, how to buy and redeem shares, what the fund's investment objectives are, and the costs involved in fund ownership.

Only load funds have sales fees, but all funds have expenses associated with operations and distribution. These charges are clearly spelled out in the fund's prospectus. The fee table explaining these charges (sometimes called 12B-1 expenses) is usually inside the prospectus' front cover. In addition to specifying the expenses as a percent of the fund's assets, there is a table that shows the dollar amount we would pay if we invested $1000 over various time periods assuming a five percent return. We should remember the five percent figure has no relationship to the return we should expect to receive. It is simply used by all funds as a standard to allow comparison on a uniform basis.

The section that spells out the objectives of the fund is also important. It tells what types of investments are included in

How to Select
Mutual Funds

Read prospectus or go to library for Morningstar or Value Line's advisory services and choose according to personal goals and objectives.

the portfolio: growth stocks, income stocks, bonds, options, or whatever. We should invest in mutual funds that share our objectives and invest in the types of companies we would select if we were to put together our own personal portfolios.

Our final review of each prospectus should note how the fund's portfolio managers have done in past years. Past performance is no guarantee of what will happen in the future. However, comparing one fund with another at least gives us some clues as to how each compared to others in the past and what we might expect in the future.

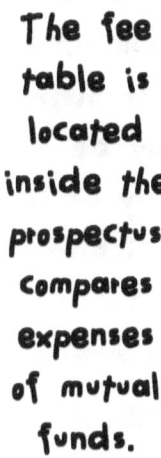

The fee table is located inside the prospectus compares expenses of mutual funds.

First, let's identify those funds that meet our objectives and match our investment preferences. As a final screen for the funds we want, we should evaluate past performance among our conservative group and find which funds look most promising. But, we should not be lured by short-term, past performance. We plan to be only long-term investors with the knowledge all investments, including mutual funds, vary in performance over a one-, two- or even five-year time frame.

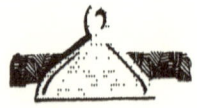

Review past 10 years performance of fund selections. while this is no guarantee, past history may be the only valid indicator of future performance.

What we want to identify are those funds that have performed consistently well over the last ten years or more. (**See** *New York Times* **May 15, 1994 clipping in Chapter 8**). Those are the ones that promise performance we should be able depend on for the long haul. The shorter term, past history of newer funds will not have enough historical data. Additionally, higher returns for the shorter period usually indicate "catching a trend" that is not easily repeated. In other words, high performance over the last year or two usually indicates a trend that will not last for the longer term. Grampa emphasizes, "*It's better to pick a fund in the top 50 over a 10-year period, than one in the top five last year.*"

It's time to compare the management fees and expenses of funds we have selected. Total expenses can vary from less than one-half of one percent to three percent or more per year based on the asset amount. The average for all funds is about 1.25%. But recognize that smaller funds, or funds with special investment costs such as international funds, may be more expensive to administer than say larger funds composed of U.S. equities only.

Consider whether higher expenses are justified by the nature or size of the fund in question. Even after selecting and purchasing a fund, we should keep track of expenses and compare them to performance to make sure expected net return is maintained.

Using this selection process, we should be able to identify three, four or five funds that are just right for us. As we will see later, we may want to identify several funds in our conservative, long-term stock fund category.

After we pick several suitable funds, there are other steps we may want to take to ensure investment success.

Grampa says it's better to choose a fund in the top 50 over a ten-year period than one in the top 5 last year.

Building a
Mutual Fund Portfolio

We have talked about the instant benefit that mutual funds provide by diversification of stock issues in various industries. But we can even take this one step further by constructing our own portfolio of mutual funds. By doing so, we are selecting a variety of investments as easily as we can in just one mutual fund. We may want the overall portfolio to contain growth stocks, small capitalization companies, index funds, etc. Each of these areas can be satisfied with a specific mutual fund. Additionally, we can incorporate different portfolio philosophies into one investment package.

No portfolio strategy works perfectly in every kind of market, but if we buy several stock funds with slightly different objectives and investment strategies, we are adding yet another dimension of diversification.

Once again, it is important to select funds that have objectives which meet our long-term investment needs and risk tolerances, and offer simplicity and ease of handling.

In early 1994, the Federal Reserve Bank raised its discount rate 1/4 of a point as a measure to contain inflationary expectations. Strange things started to happen in the bond and equity markets. As we write this, we have noted a tendency of some mutual fund managers to increase the risk in their portfolios in order to reach for higher returns. These mutual funds are anything but the conservative models of their predecessors. Some of the newer funds highlight special themes.

Even Grampa's favorite no-load fund company, Vanguard (Philadelphia, PA) has entered the contest. Although featuring close to two dozen mutual funds, Vanguard is adding an Emerging Markets Portfolio to its Vanguard International Equity Index Fund. Time will tell whether increasing risk in periods of uncertainty will pay off in higher returns. Grampa insists this is the wrong approach for us kids looking at the long-term for college tuition. These funds are shifting into selecting small capi-

In uncertain times, do not increase risks by chasing higher yields.

talized companies, corporations concentrating in foreign markets and sometimes even pricier stocks.

Since 1991, this strategy has paid off. But in riskier times this can go the other way, especially if the stock market goes into a protracted decline. Then the more aggressive funds will get hit the hardest. Grampa repeats his warning:

"In uncertain times we should not increase risks. History proves the rewards of even successful higher-risk taking is not worth the trouble."

When our personal college planning is for a 15-17 year period, an average annual compound yield of 10% will achieve our goals. Shooting for more than 10% is not necessary and certainly does not warrant increasing the risk. Grampa especially warns about the new fast-track funds promoted by even top rated mutual fund companies. Here's what prompted this curt comment in *Forbes* "Annual Mutual Fund Survey" (October 22, 1984):

"A tiny fund scorches the track, brings in big money and sends late investors into the tank."

The article describes what has come to be standard procedure for many brokerage houses and major fund organizations.

To put it in simple terms, these organizations establish "fund hatcheries" with a number of closely held funds with minimum capitalizations. These are directed by the group's managers for a period of years. The outstanding ones will be brought to the market with lots of public relations hype and advertising. The bad ones will be discarded, of course, without any publicity. The inference is that the outstanding performance of the winners is a reflection of the skill of the management company. In fact, their record may be less than mediocre. Many investors are thus lured in to buying at the top of a market cycle and unfortunately just in time to take the losses.

watch out for the scams!

Grampa says the way to avoid this fast shuffle is to always stay away from the short-term, high flyer performers of the new and smaller capitalized mutual funds, and to remember:

Read this again!

➡ **never buy last year's fashions at today's peak prices**

➡ **a smaller return over the long-term is better than a higher return over the short-term**

➡ **always stay invested without trying for "timing."**

No general discussion on mutual funds can be complete without a few words on timing geared towards beating the indexes. When stock and fund selection gets more difficult, aggressive action and greater risk-taking increases.

Market timers preach their theories on switching from fund to fund on the basis of their ability to spot the technical trends. History has proven timing to be a study in futility. According to Grampa, the long-term investor should stay fully invested all of the time. This can be hard to do, and often requires the discipline of an experienced money manager. On the other hand, more and more investment companies are setting up "index" funds. The theory is fewer and fewer money managers are doing better in the longer term than the stock market as a whole. Grampa says it's a good idea for us kids to include an index fund matching the Standard and Poor's Index 500 in our fund selection. Few funds will do better than index funds in a 15 year period.

A final word to put the concept of market timing to rest. Many parents believe there is a way to beat the market by timing. Grampa believes this is a waste of time and, more often than not, is the reason for the loss of investment opportunities because of switching too often and not being fully invested all of the time. There are many market timing advisory services and newsletters which can cost $150 and more a year. *Timer Digest* (Greenwich, Conn.), which follows 90 or more of these market timing letters, reported in April 1994 that almost 60% of these advisors were bearish on the stock market all of 1993 while prices continued to rise most of the year! Another monitor of newsletter advisory

Read Forbes 10/22/1984 article by David Dreman on scams by some major funds or brokerage houses.

The long-term investor stays fully invested all of the time.

services is the *Hulbert Financial Digest* (Alexandria, Virginia). In early 1994, the editor of this tracking organization concluded most of the advisory services over the previous five years failed to beat a simple buy and stay invested strategy. Grampa likes to say he knows some who have predicted nine of the past three bear markets! He repeats, over and over again, history has proven long-term investors should not waste their time with timing advisors or newsletters predicting the short-term course of the stock market.

Since 1925, the records prove: staying fully invested all of the time is the best course of action for us kids planning for college.

For those kids who think they are smart enough to beat the market, Grampa advises they play with the Hulbert Financial Digest to pick one or two market timing advisory services.

As for us, we stay away from short-term planning. Our principal goal is to accumulate our college funds 15 or so years from now. A long-term investing strategy is all we need. It is the only road we plan to take.

Conclusions

Eric and I believe no-load mutual funds are the best way for the average kid to attain long-term investment goals such as college, a million dollars at middle age, a special vacation after college, a comfortable retirement, or whatever suits us. This is true especially for those who cannot afford an independent money manager.

It is important to remember, even with a balanced and conservative mutual fund portfolio, there are times when we all need hand-holding and supportive advice. This is especially true in times of financial instability, when the headlines are scary. It is easy to over react and do the wrong thing at the wrong time.

Mindful of this, several funds now offer periodic services at no extra cost, advising clients when to switch within the family of funds. SteinRoe, for example, offers those with at least $50,000 invested a personal representative who will track their portfolio and call monthly or quarterly to recommend portfolio switching in

> Over the past five years, most market timing newsletters and advisory services have failed to beat the stock index funds!

Grampa
knows of
an
advisor in
market
timing
who picked
nine
of the past
three bear
markets!

accordance with their asset allocation models and specific client needs. By the way, for a free 50 page booklet, *Parent's Guide to Teaching Children About Investing,* call SteinRoe at 800-403-KIDS.

Grampa predicts ongoing guidance will soon be offered by most mutual fund companies. This service is as close as we can get to the personal guidance offered by an independent money manager. But clearly, it cannot be equivalent to the unbiased advice from a truly independent source that "wears only one hat," that of a fee-for-service professional.

It's hard to imagine a representative who receives his compensation from his mutual fund employer recommending a fund or portfolio of another company.

Presently there are more than 4000 mutual funds and a growing number of newsletters offering advice on mutual funds. Some are particularly good and reasonably priced. We prefer not to rate them or recommend any as better than the others.

This is a decision which must be based on individual and personal preferences. Since we have already mentioned several of Grampa's favorite funds and advisory services, it is only fair we present a short list of a few others. We suggest you visit the business reference section of the local library and review one or more of their mutual fund reference services such as Morningstar, Value Line Mutual Fund Survey or the No-load Fund Investor.

This should be helpful in selecting funds and those newsletters that are most suited to our personal tastes. There are excellent services available at reasonable prices, some less than $100 a year.

Summary

The
business
reference
section at
our local
library
offers
various
no-load
mutual
fund
advisory
services
and
newsletters
which can
help us
choose the
funds
appropriate
to
our personal
needs.

✔ Select only no-load stock funds with rankings in the top 50 for a period of 10 years or more.

✔ Make a decision to invest as soon as possible and establish a monthly investment program.

✔ Do not accept any more risk than necessary.

(Minimize risk even further by diversifying into several funds. Ignore cliche: _We can afford to take risks when we are young._ Remember, when we are young we need not take any larger risks. Time and the magic of compound interest is on our side.)

✔ Avoid limited partnerships and other complicated schemes.

✔ Avoid commission-earning financial advisors.

Stay away from brokers and those companies which sell products. This creates a built-in conflict of interest:

Their pocket books vs. ours

Use fee-only, professional planners whose fees are solely based on assets under management.

✔ Check performance by subscribing to at least one good no-load advisory newsletter. And let's always remember: it is perilous to make changes or to switch funds based on short-term performance.

✔ Be aware of potential changes in management of smaller no-load mutual funds. In recent years, there has been significant growth in the mutual fund industry due to increased marketing rather than good performance.

More money is being spent on advertising and selling geared to getting a larger share of the market. This could be a bad omen for those smaller funds in maintaining cost efficiency and, ultimately, their survival.

No-load funds must depend on performance because brokers do not push sales for products which by their very definition offer no commissions. There will be increased activity in mergers and acquisitions of no-load mutual funds and many will seem to have disappeared. Grampa's advice is for us to stick with the larger no-load funds that have enjoyed good performance over at least ten years and which have built their reputation on an above-average portfolio managing team. Again, watch out for those who wear more than one hat.

Ignore cliche:
" We can afford to take risks when we are young." Not true! We need take very little risk when we are young. Time and compound interest are on our side!

No-load
funds are
best for
us.

A Few Mutual Fund Advisory Services

♦ **Value Line Mutual Fund Survey**
New York, New York

♦ **Louis Rukeyser's Mutual Funds**
Alexandria, Virginia

♦ **Morningstar, Inc.***
Chicago, Illinois

♦ **No-load Fund Investor**
Irvington-on-Hudson, New York

♦ **Hulbert Guide to Financial Newsletters**
Mark Hulbert
Dearborn Financial Publishing
Chicago, Illinois

A Few No-Load Mutual Fund Investment Companies**

♦ **Dreyfus Corporation**
New York, New York

♦ **Janus Funds**
Denver, Colorado

♦ **SteinRoe**
Chicago, Illinois

♦ **T. Rowe Price Associates**
Baltimore, Maryland

♦ **Vanguard Group**
Valley Forge, Pennsylvania

But even
with good
no-load
funds,
we need
advice
periodically!

*   An independent data provider.

** For a complete list of no-load funds, refer to *The Investors
Guide to Low-Cost Mutual Funds* published by the Mutual
Fund Educational Alliance, 1900 Erie Street, Suite 120
Kansas City, Missouri 64116-3465.

CHAPTER 8
College Planning

Parents put off college planning for various reasons. Usually the rationalization goes like this:

- It's hard enough just making ends meet today. We'll begin planning for the kids college next year
- If college costs keep rising then whatever we save will hardly be enough 10-15 years from now

Without careful planning and a disciplined investment program, there is no guarantee that any family will be able to afford the increasing cost of a college education. Presently college costs are rising at more than twice the rate of inflation. The College Board, a national educational association, showed in its 1993 report, the combined costs of college increased 6%-13% depending on the type of school. There are certain steps parents should take now.

- Target school(s) of choice. The *College Cost Book* published by the College Board (Princeton, New Jersey) contains details on over 3000 colleges and universities. Determine current costs of undergraduate school and refer to Table of Projected Costs (Page103) for costs at time of future enrollment.

- Prepare an appropriate monthly investment plan. There are many groups offering detailed worksheets for constructing personal plans.

- Obtain an overview of government loan programs, scholarships and grants available, including those from private sources.

Savings for college should have
been started yesterday with
this check list:

✔ Set monthly plan   ✔ Target school(s)
✔ Scholarships   ✔ UGMA Accounts

- Establish custodial accounts in the names of the kids. The most popular as well as inexpensive way is under the Uniform Gift to Minors Act (UGMA). The advantages are principally in the ease of management and tax preferred status. There is a disadvantage: Florida (and other state) UGMAs are irrevocable transfers to the kids who take title to the account at age 18 and may use the proceeds **any way** they like, college or not. No-load mutual funds provide painless, simple plans with automatic, monthly investing.

This is Grampa's preference. Forms are provided by most all mutual funds with provisions for setting up monthly automatic transfers from checking and savings accounts.

Again, the earlier we start a planning
and savings program, the easier and safer
it is to attain our goals. As discussed in
earlier chapters, the magic of compounding increases over the longer period. A
lesser amount is required for annual savings contributions. In recent years, some
states have established programs to **guarantee** the cost of various types of admis-
sion to their universities and community
colleges.

In our state, Eric and I are eligible for
the Florida Prepaid College Program
(**FPCP**) which **guarantees** several choices
of plans at **today's tuition rate (plus an
average 6.5% surcharge).** There are
three tuition plans including:

✔ Four years at a state university
✔ Two years at a community college
✔ Two years at a community college

plus two years at a university

For those choosing four year university plans, there are also dormitory plans with flexible payment options available:

- ◆ lump sum
- ◆ five-year monthly payments until enrollment
- ◆ monthly payments

The beneficiary must be a Florida resident for twelve months and not yet in the 12th grade, or under a year old and born in Florida.

Eric and I have not decided which schools are of interest to us and whether or not we want to go to a Florida university. Our parents were born in Florida, but none except for Eric's mom went to state universities. Nevertheless, we have a feeling they'll want us to go to their alma maters in Texas, Louisiana or New Hampshire, all private schools and quite a bit more expensive than the state schools.

The **FPCP** takes these future choice problems into consideration by providing for refunds and flexibility of choice, even for private schools and out of state universities. The

program is guaranteed by the Florida legis-
lature and the State of Florida. Refunds are
provided for unused credits and the following options are provided:

The cost of
4 years of college
+ 2 years of
dormitory expenses
for both Eric &
Elizabeth can be
handled for
only $161.
per month!

Prepaid benefits may be:

♦ transferred to a sibling

♦ cancelled with full refund*

♦ transferred to an <u>in-state</u> private col-
    lege or university

♦ transferred to an <u>out-of-state</u> college
    or university** that is accredited and
    not-for-profit

For purposes of this planning exercise,
which is to provide funds for college, let's
first consider the Florida Prepaid College
Plan. What's there to lose? We can thus
guarantee four years of college and an option to go to private colleges either in or
outside of Florida. And we can do this at
**today's tuition rates (plus an average
6.5% surcharge)!**

*   Less an administrative fee. No interest will be refunded.
**   The lesser of current rate at Florida public institutions, or the original
     purchase price plus five percent interest compounded annually after
     assessment of a $25 transfer fee. (Master Covenant 1993-1994)

Eric and I are Florida residents since we were born in the state in 1991 and 1993. For simplicity's sake, we will opt for monthly payments for four years of university tuition and two years* of a prepaid dormitory contract.

According to the tables provided, these are the monthly** payments required to cover these costs in the years 2010 and 2009 respectively for Eric and me:

Eric $79
Elizabeth $82

Eric says several states have similar guaranteed, prepaid programs. He has been told by our accountant of instances where parents are receiving tax notices from the Internal Revenue Service. Apparently, the increase in value of current year tuition over guaranteed costs in year of enrollment in the FPCP is considered income by the IRS. The good news remains: this increase in value is paid by the state of Florida, but considered

Eric says: Never let the tax tail wag the dog.

* Dormitory contracts for only one year, which is more common, would reduce overall costs by approximately 25%.
** These monthly payments begin April 1994 and continue until October 2010 for Eric and until October 2009 for Elizabeth.

taxable income in the year of payment for federal tax purposes.

Pay your money to FPcP and take your chances.

Nevertheless, Grampa approves of the concept because, at the very least, it provides for a full college program at **today's tuition rate (plus an average 6.5 % surcharge).** Even if we should decide to go to colleges more expensive than state universities, and are fortunate enough to have the additional funds, the **FPCP** funds will be in place to cover part of the costs. And most important of all, the **FPCP** can make college readily affordable to all families willing to prioritize their budgets for this most important item in family planning. The Florida plan even makes provisions for insuring the provider as a further guarantee to have the funds in place when the children are ready to enroll.

Grampa told us he had a more sophisticated college program in place before he learned of the **FPCP.** Because he likes the guaranteed cost feature of Florida college, he decided to **also** enroll us in the **FPCP.** Eric's dad, however, is not overly thrilled with the prospects of **FPCP.**

Uncle Steve appreciates the feeling of security of guaranteeing college at **today's**

tuition rate (plus an average 6.5 % sur-charge). But he is skeptical of government guarantees and says, *"Anything that looks too good to be true **is usually** too good to be true."* So Uncle Steve did some research and found a cover story in the January 10, 1992 edition of the *Miami Review* (now the *Daily Business Review*).

In this three-page feature article, doubts were raised as to the validity and reliability of the general assumptions made in the plan. The basic assumption forecasting state college tuition increases at 7.5% a year for the next decade is already in doubt. For the first three years, tuition increases have already been 8%, 10% and 15%. If that trend continues, the FPCP fund could be substantially insufficient precisely when, at the turn of the century, the largest number of contracted students plan to enter as freshmen.

The state of Florida has reserved the right to kill the program outright. Their guarantee amounts to a firm promise only to refund the money to participants with interest only at passbook savings rates.

If it sounds too good to be true, it probably is too good to be true!

The FPCP further assumes the trustee for the funds, U.S. Trust in New York, will be able to earn a return of 8.5 % per year on the investment portfolio. If these assumptions go awry, the only capital backing is the promise of the State of Florida.

FPCP should still be a Corner- stone for College planning!

There has been a huge registration for FPCP and, what initially appears to be an overwhelming success, may have serious and contrary results.

Forgetting for a moment the potential for financial problems, let us assume FPCP registration will continue at the predicted rate. Uncle Steve asks what, then, happens if most of the kids in the program choose to go to a few of the more popular schools?

Obviously, the overflow would be directed to the other state colleges. For example, if Florida International University could not accept any more students in a freshman class, the overflow would be assigned to another school, let's say, the University of West Florida at Pensacola.

South Florida students (and families alike) might not be too pleased about going to a school, not of choice, 500 miles away. This is where the "guarantee" would most probably be triggered. The FPCP would be compelled to repay the principal invested plus only the accumulated interest at the prevailing passbook interest rate. Something to think about!

If the FPCP works, however, it is still the only program we know of that is seriously dealing with guaranteed college for Florida residents and, as such, should be taken seriously as a foundation for initial college planning, especially for those of us with families of more modest financial means. Grampa reasons:

All plans of mice, men and even grandchildren can change. Nobody is guaranteed anything in life.

Uncle Steve acknowledged the wisdom of his dad's thesis and agreed: **FPCP should be the cornerstone of initial college planning.** (For information, call 800-552-4723).

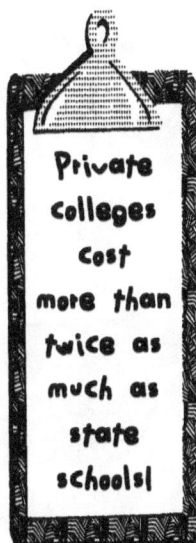

Uncle Steve did some additional research, examining the data released by the College Board for the period 1993-1994. College costs were:

$6,759 for state schools

$16,374 for private schools

Assuming an average, annual rate of increase in college costs of seven percent, Uncle Steve prepared a projection of future college costs. Eric is now one year old and should enter the college of his choice in 17 years (2010). I am two and should start college in 2009 or 16 years from now. This is an estimate, of course, assuming entrance age at 18.

We should also remember that the entire cost of college does not have to be ready and available at the time of registration as freshmen. We need to pay only for first-year costs in 16 or 17 years. Meanwhile, our funds continue to accumulate for the next three years as current annual payments are required.

Can you believe it will cost more than $300,000 to send one kid, born in 1999 or after, to a private college?

Projected College Costs
(Four Years)
1996 to 2010

Current Age	Years until college begins	Public College	Private College
(Eric)1	17	$ 94,795	$ 229,645
(Eliz)2	16	$ 88,593	$ 214,621
3	15	$ 82,797	$ 200,581
4	14	$ 77,381	$ 187,548
5	13	$ 72,318	$ 175,195
6	12	$ 67,587	$ 163,733
7	11	$ 63,166	$ 153,022
8	10	$ 59,033	$ 143,011
9	9	$ 55,171	$ 133,655
10	8	$ 51,562	$ 124,911
11	7	$ 48,189	$ 116,740
12	6	$ 45,036	$ 109,103
13	5	$ 42,090	$ 101,965
14	4	$ 39,336	$ 95,294
15	3	$ 36,763	$ 89,060

Uncle Steve figures Eric alone would require $72,700 at today's costs to fund four years of college. Uncle Steve's calculation assumes an average 7% annual increase in college costs. In the year 2010, Eric would need $229,645.

(See table of Projected College Costs 1996-2010)

It is difficult to believe: almost a quarter of a million dollars is needed for just one kid's college costs! Uncle Steve also calculates the cost of college for kids born in 1999 or later will increase to more than $300,000. It doesn't take a mathematical genius to realize few families can afford to send even one child to college at these prices. These numbers are mind-boggling to most and one more reason so few people are ready to tackle the problems of planning for the future.

Availability of student loans should continue to increase well into the 21st century to supplement even the best made college plans.

It is also the reason for the geometric growth of the student loan industry. Statistics from the U.S. Department of Education revealed in 1993 that loans totalled $19.7 billion, an increase of more than 25% over 1992! Loans in 1994 and thereafter should continue to increase significantly due to several factors:

- ◆ Legislative changes have resulted in a raising of loan limits to students, including those in graduate schools. Some of these caps have been increased by as much as 50%.

- ◆ Affluent students (i.e., those who "flunk" the financial-need test) have become eligible for student loans. This alone has resulted in loan increases of almost 25% from 1992.

◆ Loan caps have been removed from parent loan programs. Previously parents had a limit of $4000 a year. Now they can borrow the full amount of the difference between their children's total education expenses and their financial assistance packages.

Home values are no longer considered part of the family net worth in computing eligibility for financial aid. This is important for families who are "house rich" but without sufficient liquid assets to qualify for college loans.

Grampa, Uncle Steve and my folks consider borrowing from colleges and the government a last resort and only for those who have put off planning, or have not planned too well and must supplement savings with financial aid.

Their primary goal still is to get started on serious college planning as soon as possible, maybe even before the kids are born.

EQUITY in a house is no longer considered part of parent's net worth in meeting the financial-need test for student loans.

Let's remember to tell our folks to get started with our college planning as soon as possible !

Special college funding products are now offered by the financial services industry featuring tuition guarantees.

The CollegeSure CD* offered by the College Savings Bank of Princeton, New Jersey appears to go further than the FPCP. It offers a federally insured, long-term investment plan with a return that is tied to the average cost of a college education. Like the FPCP, this private savings bank offers both a savings plan and insurance in the form of a guarantee against inflation in future college costs.

A CollegeSure CD is a Federal Deposit Insurance Corporation (FDIC) insured certificate of deposit (CD) backed by the full faith and credit of the United States up to $100,000 for each depositor. After the minimum initial investment of $1000, addi-

* For more info on the CollegeSure CD program call 800-888-2723.

tional purchases may be made in whole units or fractions of a unit under a variety of automatic savings plans.

> One single unit is guaranteed at maturity (one to five years) to pay no less than the average cost of one year's tuition, fees, room and board at the average private college in the U.S.

The College Board prepares an annual index of college costs of the largest 500 private colleges in the country which is published July 31 each year. This Independent College Index shows the percentage rate of change over the prior year (i.e., the college-cost-inflation factor) which forms the foundation of College Saving's guarantee. Each year, the bank adds to each CD this inflation factor less its 1-1.5% margin. However, the College Savings Bank guarantees payment of no less than four percent annually regardless of the rate of college inflation.

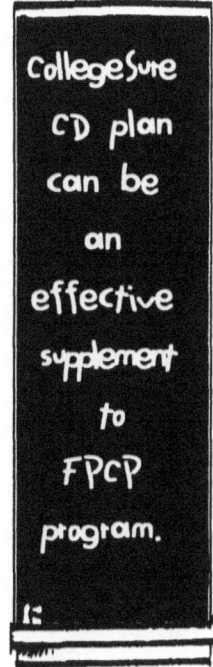

CollegeSure CD plan can be an effective supplement to FPCP program.

If a decision is made at maturity to forget about college, whatever the reason, the funds are released with the accumulated earnings. However, as with most CDs, withdrawal before maturity carries penalties as high as 10%.

There may be several less attractive features in the CollegeSure CD program. Treasury notes have performed better historically. On the other hand, "T" notes do not guarantee future college costs. A more serious consideration is if inflation and the cost of college rise well beyond projections while interest rates stay at current lower levels, the CollegeSure CD program may not be in a position to continue its program. This is an inherent problem of all CD funds in times of rising inflation.

Uncle Steve reminds us that in periods where inflation appears to be dormant, or at least under control, CDs and other money instruments become more popular. Uncle Steve and Grampa insist inflation is merely taking a breather and will soon be a factor to be again seriously reckoned with. It is also the reason why Eric prefers to invest in no-load mutual stock funds. In the long-term, stocks have outperformed CDs and "T" notes by more than 2:1. And, as Eric says, "Our college plan is clearly for the longer term."

Uncle Steve is the director of a portfolio management company in South Florida which emphasizes there has been no better scenario in the past 69 years than to have been an investor in the stocks of U.S. companies **(See Chapter 1).** From 1925 to the present, stocks have clearly outperformed CDs, Treasury notes and bonds by more than 2:1.*

Let's return to Uncle Steve's calculations for Eric's college costs. He believes in the magic of compounding and monthly investing of a budgeted sum into either of his two favorite no-load stock mutual funds:

At our age, college planning is strictly a long-term deal.

> ✔ Vanguard Index 500
> or
> ✔ Vanguard Windsor II

Since Eric needs a 17 year program, Uncle Steve feels there is sufficient time to invest a calculated monthly sum into this fund for about 14 or 15 years and, with timing, depending on the then state of the stock market, transfer the total amount into CollegeSure **Plus** CDs. In this way, Eric should not have to depend on the possible illiquidity of the stock market in the year 2010.

---

* Editor's Note: The reiteration of this statistic is not accidental. Hopefully, it will be adopted as a well-intended mantra, committed to memory and spread as gospel to all our serious, long-term investor friends.

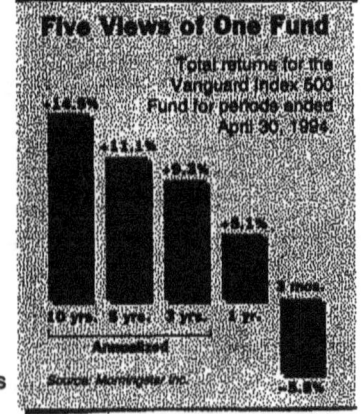

Uncle
Steve's
plan for
investing
$433
a month for
17 years at
a projected
annual
return of
10% to
produce the
$230,000
required
for Eric's
college looks
even better
after
Morningstar's
report!

Uncle Steve plans to look carefully at the market factors beginning in 2007 in order to allow for an unrushed and properly timed exit from the mutual fund.

He expects to have enough time to transfer the major portion of Eric's tuition to the CollegeSure **Plus** CD which offers a higher interest rate than the CollegeSure CD.

Uncle Steve calculates a monthly investment of $433, with a compound annual growth rate of 10% will produce a fund of $230,000 for Eric in the year 2010! Even with a transfer two to three years earlier to the CollegeSure program, Uncle Steve figures this to be a reasonable and conservative estimate.

The May 15, 1994, edition of the *New York Times** published Morningstar Inc.'s report on periodic returns of Vanguard Index 500 Fund:

* Copyright © 1994 by the New York Times Company. Reprinted by permission. See also p.150 for 15-year averages compiled by Morningstar, Inc.

Five Views of One Fund

Total returns for the Vanguard Index 500 Fund for periods ended April 30, 1994.

It is interesting to note while the Vanguard Index Fund achieved a total return
of 14.5% for the ten year period ending
April 30, 1994, the company's Wellington
Fund achieved almost the same results at
14.6%. And, even more interesting is the
20-year total return of the Vanguard
Group's equity funds all of which managed
to achieve more than the 10% average annual return required by Eric's dad, Steve.

With this April 30, 1994, update of the
10-year performance record of 14.5% of Vanguard Index 500 Fund, and Ibbottson Associates reporting of the 68-year record of the
average annual growth of equities to be in
excess of 10% (See Chapter 1), Uncle Steve
feels comfortable using his estimated 10%
rate in calculations for our long-term planning. History is no guarantee of what the
future will bring, but the historical average
interest rate gives us the best measuring
stick available for future projections.

After reviewing this with my and Eric's
parents, Grampa proposed to establish two
Florida gift to minors trusts, one for each of
us. My mom is to be custodian for mine and
Eric's mom for his. He opened the two ac-

Average
Stock Yields
(with invested
dividends)

→ 10.3% over
68 years
(Ibbotson
Associates)

→ 14.5% over
10 years
(N.Y. Times
5/15/94)

→ 14.57%
over 15 years
(See Morning
Star Inc.
report on
page 152)

counts Under the Florida Uniform Gift to Minors Act (UGMA) in the Index 500 Fund of the Vanguard Group with an opening deposit of $1000 for each of us. Grampa (and Grandma) have made arrangements beginning in September 1994 for monthly payments of $500 to each of the UGMA accounts for Eric and me. In effect, these are gifts to us grandkids which are within the combined annual gift tax exclusion of Grampa and Grandma. Sticking to our family's firm belief in diversification, Grampa expects to open additional equity accounts in the Vanguard Group starting with Windsor II after several years and rotating the monthly contributions within the group.

Based on Grampa's and Steve's calculations, Eric and I should have funds of more than the total projected costs of college for 2009 and 2010. If, however, the historical assumptions for the average 10% growth do not hold up, at the very least, there should be ample sums available for the payment of tuition for most of the four year undergraduate programs of other good private universities.

Of course there's always the student government loan program as a backup. For information, call 800-4-FED-AID.

Grampa frowns on overreliance on loans except for minimum supplementation. We should try our best to finish college and begin our careers and family life without the initial burden of too much debt. According to him, this is one of the major obstacles to successful financial and investment planning. He prefers some of the other alternatives.

Let's first review the prospects of investing lesser amounts. This is especially important to those who simply cannot afford to lay away $500 per month. Following is a table measuring the college funds which should be accumulated over various periods with smaller monthly payments.

Long-term college planning will keep our families out of the poor house.

**PROJECTED FUND ACCUMULATION
FOR MONTHLY PAYMENTS OVER
VARIOUS PERIODS OF YEARS**

Monthly Payment	10 Years	12 Years	14 Years	17 Years
$100.00	$20,480.00	$27,636.00	$36,369.00	$53,203.00
$200.00	$40,960.00	$55,272.00	$72,737.00	$106,407.00
$300.00	$61,439.00	$82,908.00	$109,106.00	$159,610.00
$400.00	$81,919.00	$110,544.00	$145,474.00	$212,800.00
$500.00	$102,399.00	$138,180.00	$181,843.00	$266,017.00

Other Plans

It is not hard to understand the importance of early planning for the kids' college for most families, rich or poor. Based on the aforementioned projected costs, it may even be more urgent for the so-called rich or well-to-do. Private colleges may have to take into consideration various options to deal with this. If escalating costs are not more strictly controlled, or more financing programs made available, private colleges could experience severe drops in enrollment by the early 21st century. Certainly those schools with tuition increments of two to three times the increase of the annual inflation rate will have to do some sober reviewing and recalculating.

Parents should contact their colleges of choice early on and request information as to their financial aid, scholarship and grants programs. As with all businesses, colleges and universities must be competitive and do some intensive marketing to attract their customers. Most colleges have sophisticated financial assistance and scholarship programs in place. If and when we need to supplement our funds with college loans, I suppose we'll begin by choosing several of the books listed at the end of this chapter. For sure, we won't tell Grampa, who is proud to say that the only consumer loans he ever made were for home mortgages!

Guaranteeing future tuition and other college costs is a concept that should be further developed especially when rising inflation again becomes more of a problem. We must remember, there is a cost to guar-

Grampa's recommendation:

Guarantee state college costs with FPCP plus regular investing in a no-load mutual fund program.

antees, whether offered by state programs such as FPCP, or private ones such as CollegeSure CDs.

And there are other considerations, pro and con of each program, that should be carefully evaluated. Grampa recommends careful attention to combining "guarantee" plans with supplementary no-load stock funds. Uncle Steve agrees.

We kids, and our families, must make choices in accordance with personal circumstances. What is good for some may not be attainable for others. When costs of private colleges go into the stratospheric areas of $300,000 and up per kid, it becomes clear that community colleges may offer the best of all worlds to some families, especially those for whom Ivy League schools are not a priority.

Families where mom and dad must both work and are on tight budgets may well have to forego planning for expensive private colleges.

Athletic, academic and other scholarships have become part of long range planning for many. It is a subject not covered in this chapter. Books have been recently

★ ★ ★

Contact your local recruiting office for info on GI Bill college benefit programs.

published on this subject listing the various scholarships offered by private and public sources.

Our parents say they know people who have "programmed" their kids into special college pursuits. One, a friend of my mom, heard that the school of her choice, a private university in the Midwest, was offering full scholarships to students who play the tuba and oboe. Know what she did for her two kids? You guessed right. She started them in music lessons for tuba and oboe! They tried out for the high school orchestra and marching band and made it. Both later received full scholarships to the college in the Midwest!

Most of us know how intense the competition is for high school athletic stars especially in football and basketball. But how many of us are aware of scholarships offered for tennis, gymnastics, wrestling and high diving?

And, lest we forget, there's always the opportunity for those who qualify to enlist in United States Armed Forces where certain enlistment terms will qualify for GI Bill paid college benefits. Information is readily available from each branch of the military.

Parents might also consider starting their research for lists of available scholarships at the reference desk at their local library. Check the books and information available on private and public funded scholarship and grant programs.

As we go to press, statistics reveal college students are taking out loans in record numbers. Nationally, students borrowed $7.8 billion from October 1993 through March 1994. This equals an increase of 44% over the same period the year before.

More info for getting us our college money . . .

A Few Good Books and Other Sources for Getting Money for College

♦ **Get Real**
*A Students Guide to Money & Other
Practical Matters
by Tenuto and Schwartzwald
Harcourt Brace Jovanovich
Orlando, Florida*

♦ **Grants, Loans and Work
Study**
*The Students Guide to Financial Aid
from the U.S. Department of
Education*

♦ **Free Money for College**
*A Guide to More than 1000 Grants
and Scholarships for Undergraduate
Study
Laurie Blum
Facts on File Inc.
New York, N.Y.*

♦ **Free Money for Athletic
Scholarships**

♦ **Free Money for College
from the Government**

♦ **Free Money from Colleges
and Universities**
*Henry Holt and Company
New York, N.Y.*

Here's

some

more

good

reading.

♦ ***Student Guide to Paying for College***
Financial Aid and Financial Planning: The Most Effective System for Cutting College Costs Regardless of Your Income
by Chany and Martz
Villard Books
New York, N.Y.

♦ ***Winning Money for College***
The High School Student's Guide to Scholarship Contests
by Alan Deutschman
Peterson's Guides
Princeton, New Jersey

♦ ***Cash for College***
The Ultimate Guide to College Scholarships
by McKee and McKee
Hearst Books
New York

♦ ***The Scholarship Book***
About Grants and Private-Sector Funds
by Daniel Cassidy
Prentice Hall
Englewood Cliffs, New Jersey

CHAPTER 9
A Few More Tips

As you must have already noted, this book is not meant to serve as a compleat desk top reference for investing. There are many worthy books on the market covering all aspects of investing as well as financial planning.

Our main purpose is to offer a "user-friendly" primer that focuses on the need for action and an early start in investing. This should provide the foundation for a calm, unhurried program over a long-term period with meaningfully lower risk-taking to achieve our goals.

Additionally, we have focused on simplicity in planning and the strict independence of our advisors. We have also concentrated on being wary of scams and of those who make glamorous if not realistic promises. If the marketing story or advertisement sounds too good to be true, it usu-

This book should serve as a

*

Primer on long-term investing

*

Guide for college planning

*

Guide for simplicity in planning

*

Scam and "free" tip alert

*

Reference for independent investment sources

watch out for the hucksters!

ally is too good to be true. When the self-acclaimed advisor offers free advice, remember **there is no free lunch** in investing. Those who sell products typically do not charge for their advice. They earn their livelihood from commissions earned.

In the stock brokerage industry, commissions are earned when we buy and also when we sell. In the past few years, some brokerage companies have begun to "double-dip" by establishing separate divisions offering portfolio management for a fee. In many cases these divisions are staffed with accredited professionals.

Even so, Grampa insists we deal only with **independent** firms. Because of this, he no longer recommends the pioneer company Fidelity Investments which started up 48 years ago as a load (i.e., front-end commission) family of funds sold only by brokers. In 1979, Fidelity switched to direct selling (i.e., without outside brokers) and offered a variety of no-load funds. Today it is the country's largest privately held mutual fund and discount brokerage company. It offers investors more than 180 mutual funds, insurance products, Treasury bills, certificates of deposit and individual securities. In 1994, Fidelity again reversed its course and now offers funds sold exclusively through outside brokers. In addition to its funds and discount brokerage services, Fidelity Advisors, a division of the parent company, now charges portfolio advisory fees up to 4.75% of assets managed. They also charge fees for marketing and distribution to pay outside brokers for their services.

So what's wrong with this? Grampa acknowledges, while it is not illegal to work both sides of the street or to wear more than one hat, Fidelity Advisors is not truly **independent** and therefore should not offer **independent professional portfolio advisory services.** Grampa insists independent services can best be offered by qualified companies that wear only one hat and walk only on only one side of the street.

Grampa asked Eric and me to prepare a list of his tips to conclude this final chapter. Eric offered to list the tips in alphabetical order although not necessarily in order of priority or importance. Here's what he came up with. . .

Always be wary of financial "professionals" and consultants whose only credentials are their advertisements in church, Rotary, Kiwanis, Lions, etc. bulletins. Watch out for the self-styled financial service professionals and investment consultants with insurance licenses and those working for companies selling financial products.

Tip: Ask the family CPA or lawyer to recommend a qualified, independent professional. Remember, professionals rarely make unsolicited, "cold" telephone calls.

Conclusions and Grampa's tips as translated by Eric.

Beware of grim media and newsletter advice which encourages bailing out of or switching stock funds. Usually the best time to buy is when everybody yells "sell." This is when it is indispensable to heed the advice of a competent, independent, professional advisor.

Consider reviewing a semi-monthly publication initiated in 1992 by Morningstar Inc. It has a special feature which lists three (3) funds with similarities to the fund being profiled. This splendid function offers no-load substitutes for load funds. Also where funds are closed, it lists alternative funds that are similar and open to new investors.

> **Tip:** Most local public libraries have this service available to the public.

Don't believe any new programs and "good deals" until they are checked out by a respected advisory service such as *Morningstar *Value Line or *No-Load Fund Investor

Don't rush to new programs offered by various brokerage houses where they offer to sell no-load funds without initial cost to new customers. While they offer the advantage of one-stop shopping, there are less obvious disadvantages. One is in losing direct contact with the funds and in relying on the brokerage house for total (but not independent) management.

> **Tip:** Be alert to the potential conflict of interest where the brokerage company includes its own funds in the packages offered.

Euphemisms can be dangerous. Watch out for the high-yield or high-income funds. They might better be called high-

risk funds. Almost without exception, these funds do not belong in our long-term investment programs. A new addition to the games in yield stretching is the controversial speculation using "derivatives." (See **"K"** below.)

> Tip: With long-term equity investing the risk we need is minimal. As young folks, we <u>cannot afford to take risks</u>, especially if the additional risk is not necessary to fulfill our goals.

young folks need not accept high risks! Time is on our side for low-risk investing!

Forgo incurring excessive consumer debt. In the early 1960s, the now defunct Pan American Airlines had a slogan: "Fly now, pay later." This may be good for airline revenues but its a bad habit for us. What can be more painful than paying for the next year for an already forgotten vacation in Jamaica? Consumer debt should be limited to those items that are still around as we pay the debt off, such as home mortgages and car loans. Unlike vacations, cars and homes have continuing utility.

> Tip: Having a low debt balance can really look good when it's time for college loans.

G et more information on the "new kids on the block" mutual funds. Presently there are more than 4000 mutual funds with new ones forming almost every week, offering exotic promises. Check on the "good deals" with Dun & Bradstreet, telephone 800-362-2255. Reports are available on a company's history and background, payment records, finances, lawsuits, liens and judgments. The National Association of Security Dealers (NASD) will provide a summary report of the disciplinary history of someone in the brokerage industry.

Tip: For information call the NASD at 800-289-9999.

H ard currency, certificates of deposit (CDs) and Treasury bills should not to be considered more conservative or safe than putting our money in cookie jars. Be aware of what inflation risk can do to our nest egg. When we put our money in the bank or in Treasury bills, the backing of the full faith and credit of the U.S. may help us sleep over the short-term. However, over longer periods, CDs earning 2.5% aren't a very good deal with an annual inflation rate at three percent or more.

Tip: Except for limited, special short-term use, CDs are not recommended.

Inflation can have a huge impact on our investment planning. A rate of about seven percent a year, in just 10 years, will cut a dollar's purchasing power in half!

Tip: Grampa recommends keeping most of our investments in quality equity portfolios and mutual funds. Bonds are also not an inflation hedge!

Money in the bank, CD's and bonds do not protect us from inflation risk!

Judgement time comes with initial college registration and enrollment for the evaluation of accumulated funds. Fortunately, only first year college tuition and costs need to be available. Hopefully, our fund accumulation will be on target. Otherwise this would be a good time to make alterations to the investment strategy and also look again at the current options for student aid and work-study programs.

Tip: There are excellent reference books available. (See listing in Chapter 8).

Know there are no gurus smart enough to forecast or predict the market (not even Grampa). Beware of those who say they can time the market. Market timers are like tea-leaf readers and fortune-tellers according to Grampa who says they wouldn't be hawking their newsletters if they could do what they say. They would already be rich enough to spend all their time forecasting weather conditions for world cruises on their private yachts. Leave complex investing out of our game plans. We should invest in things we can understand, and deal with only those advisors who make things easy to understand. And let's not forget **K-I-S-S**:

There are some good reference books in the public library.

KEEP IT SIMPLE SMARTY

We must remember to stay invested in established, non-trendy, no-load stock funds and to stay clear of limited partnerships and complicated schemes. As an example, stay away from those funds which attempt to stretch their yields by investing in the current scheme called derivatives. These are highly risky and can produce big returns. Unfortunately, they also produce big losses.

Ignore the complicated deals of the market timers!

Derivatives are simply speculations, usually between two parties betting on the performance of some agreed benchmark such as stock options or futures.

Check exposure to high-risk derivatives!

Grampa warns us these are usually the signposts of speculative risk and excessive volatility. His advice is to stay away from those funds and advisors who invest even portions of their portfolios in derivatives.

In a *Wall Street Journal* news item on July 23, 1994, PaineWebber disclosed it would spend $180 million to bail out a mutual fund battered by its holdings of the highly technical and often risky Wall Street securities called derivatives.

when in doubt call the fund companies and ask about their derivative exposure. It may be worthwhile to check with Morningstar,Inc. for their checklist of mutual funds with sizeable holdings of derivatives.

To boot, Grampa warns about recent tendencies of some advisors to recommend investing in other short-term distractions as overseas and small stock funds. They rationalize this by claiming this increases diversification. Their ads promise higher yield without much more risk.

The reality comes sooner than expected. Some companies and their "independent" advisors pitched short-term bond funds as ultrasafe. Their ads never mentioned the possible loss of principal which did in fact occur in the spring of 1994 when some of these "ultrasafe" funds lost more than 16% of their value. In their aggressive marketing, these funds extolled the virtues of their holdings in U.S. government paper as if Treasuries and government bonds were immune to declines.

> Tip: While investments may decline over the short-term, it's over the long-term where risk distinctions are best evaluated.

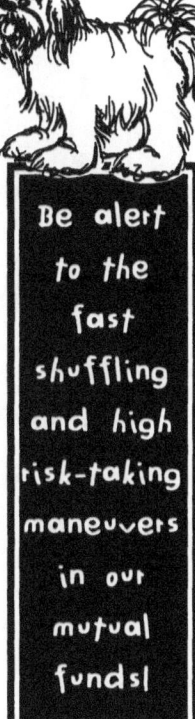

Lower management fees mean lower overhead and, as with no-load funds, this translates into more dollars working for **us**. Even no-loads have varying overhead costs. There are several no-load funds that concentrate on keeping their costs down. It makes good sense to watch fund costs. Over the long-term, this can add up to significant returns. Check with the No Load Fund Investor or Morningstar to keep an eye on the overhead of favorite funds. *Consumer Reports*, also available at the reference section of most local libraries, offers easy to understand, no-load fund comparisons and recommendations.

Be alert to the fast shuffling and high risk-taking maneuvers in our mutual funds!

It is worth noting the current focus of some of the no-load funds on Grampa's list of favorites. Simply, their priority is to limit the number of short-term trades. Fewer trades result in lower costs of management as well as lower capital gains taxes, both beneficial to the bottom line of the individual investor. Value Line Mutual Fund Survey offers a new service in 1994 which focuses on the above features. It includes a biweekly packet and updates three times a year on 2000 mutual funds. Among the new features prominently displayed are:

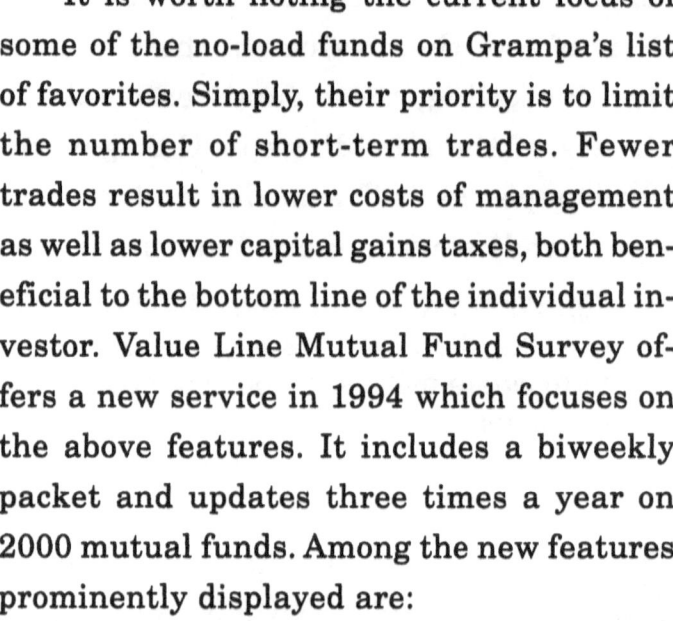

Keep an eye on management costs!

- Its measurement of how much of the portfolio's value is represented by gains on unsold stocks. When sold these stocks would generate taxes to investors.

- Its listing of all relevant fees and management expenses.

- Its display of fund performance versus the amount of assumed risk.

- Its listing of the results of a $10,000 investment for as long as 15 years compared to its peer group and the Standard and Poor's 500 Index .

Tip: We suggest a review of management costs every two years.

Make sure to stay away from sector or single industry funds. Putting most of our eggs in one basket can defeat our need to minimize risk over the longer term via diversifying our holdings into a broader selection of companies and industries.

> Tip: Investing in two or three funds helps in comparing management costs and fees.

Things we like to see in our mutual funds

* limited amount of trades

* lower management costs

* lower marketing fees

Never allow market-timing strategies to temporarily switch us out of fund holdings. History and documented data prove it's a better strategy to always stay fully invested.

A program of regular periodic additions to our investment portfolio offers the extra advantage of dollar-cost averaging. Isn't it a good idea to buy needed school supplies when they are on sale and selling for less? For example, if we need lots of paper pads which sell for one dollar each, wouldn't it be a good idea to buy several dozen or so when they're on sale for 60 cents each?

On the other hand, timing may become an important consideration to guarantee liquidity of stock funds prior to the time to make initial college tuition payments. This is another decision best left to the professionals who may suggest switching the appropriate amounts from the no-load stock funds to more liquid money market funds or CDs. (Note Chapter 8 and discussion of the CollegeSure CD Plan.)

Tip: Take advantage of market drops (bargains?) to increase holdings in favorite funds.

we never should put all our eggs in one basket.

Overreaction to stock market "panics" and excess media reaction can result in anxiety-triggered, bad decisions. When the market sends nervous signals, too many good plans of mice and men can go astray.

Mutual funds accounted for 84% of all shares acquired in 1992. In 1993, fund purchases increased by 125% with no signs of slowdown in 1994. It is clear: mutual fund activity has become the driving force in the stock market. Investment experts have become concerned about potential sell-offs by mutual fund investors, especially those who are not, by definition, long-term investors.

The volume of daily trading has increased geometrically. Any sell-off encouraged by nervous selling could produce a scary drop in fund values. It stands to reason, if we are in for the long-term, we must avoid panic decisions made in reaction to short-term bad news. This is easier said and read than done. But Grampa tells us the most important thing is to have access to independent, professional advice which should reduce the potential for panic selling. And he urges all of us to keep in mind: **Drops over the short-term are the nature of the stock market but over the long term, quality equities do better than any other form of security!**

A focus on long-term investment planning will eliminate short-term panic!

> Tip: As others panic, savvy long-term investors do best by staying inside when the heavy winds hit. Smart kids wait before they go outside to play.

Payment for hidden expenses and costs of marketing "no-load" funds has become pervasive. In a previous section (See

Be alert to the hidden "loads" in no-load funds.

Keep cool and in touch with a calm and independent advisor.

Section "L"), the lowering of management fees is discussed. The subject of hazy management and marketing costs gets confusing as more of the old line "load" companies continue to withdraw from the increasingly unpopular front loading funds. Instead they now offer a barrage of so-called, no-load funds.

"Here they go again!" Grampa warns. In 1994, Fidelity Funds added 129 no-load funds to their one-stop network, now totalling 327 so-called no-load funds. Prudential Securities also joined this trend in 1994 and switched to selling no-load funds.

Let's examine what no-load really means and take a clear look at what constitutes hidden marketing fees and other expenses of management. We are trying not to scare everybody as we explain in simple terms what has become more complicated every year.

We will have succeeded if readers gain enough knowledge of the true no-load costs investors pay. Simply, no-load funds are no guarantee that we are paying less for marketing and management.

Here's a summary of the different types of loads and expenses:

Loads (i.e., direct sales commissions) may be front load or back load.

Front load: The sales charge is taken off the initial investment. Depending on the amount of investment, this front end commission varies from 2.5% to 5.5%. For example, a $10,000 fund investment with a 5% front load would have $9500 left.

Back load: There is no commission taken when buying shares in the fund, but there is an "exit" charge usually varying between 4% and 6% that phases out in five or more years.

Loads by another name are the not-so-obvious, marketing fees called the section 12(b)-1 fees.

These are annual fees paid to selling brokers. Ranging up to 1%, they are paid each and every year. Simply stated: in five years, this could be more costly to the long-term investor than a 4% front load fund! Grampa likes to compare this situation of labeling distinctions of sales commissions,

Aggressive marketers can be dangerous to our financial health !

i.e., loads vs. 12(b)-1 expenses by para-
phrasing the memorable lines from Romeo
and Juliet:

What's in a name?
That which we call a rose
By any other name
would smell as sweet.

As Grampa puts it,

"A load is a load
even when called
a 12(b)-1 expense
in a so-called,
no-load fund."

In order to keep an eye on all management fees and costs; it is important to know the differences in front and back loads and Section 12(b)-1 fees!

The new Value Line Mutual Fund Survey clearly and prominently displays the expense structure of each fund with this breakdown:

◆ management fee

◆ 12(b)-1 fee

◆ initial load

Tip: Grampa insists this service alone is worth the cost of a subscription or at least a biannual visit to the public library.

Questions should be asked before buying how-to-invest books even from best-seller lists. We often hear about readers feeling intimidated and overwhelmed by financial books. Some books, indeed, are loaded with jargon and fancy words.

Others may be easier to read. These may be suspect just because they do make too-easy reading. These books may have been written by writers with more skills in marketing than in finance and investing. They even manage, at times, to make the best seller lists. Simply, these people know how to sell anything including money

Here are some tips on a few reference books and sensible reading.

books. Recently, a best selling author was indicted for fraud and sued for megabucks. Grampa warns us again against the get-rich-quick theme books.

He says the best books may have been written by the ladies. In 1975, it was Sylvia Porter who wrote the best overall, how-to-invest book. Published by Doubleday, the *Sylvia Porter Money Book* with its 1105 pages sold for $12.50. It still serves as an encyclopedic family finance reference book after all these years. The current Sylvia Porter book, *Planning Your Retirement,* has 262 pages, is published by Prentice Hall and sells for $16.

In 1991 another good reference book with only 934 pages was published by Simon and Schuster. Jane Bryant Quinn, the author, upholds the reputation of the ladies in her book, *Making the Most of Your Money*. It should serve well those in need of a fine home reference source. At a price of $27.50, it reflects the effects of inflation but it is easily worth the cost.

For those interested only in the refinements of mutual fund investing, Grampa recommends *Bogle on Mutual Funds* published by Irwin Professional Publishing. John Bogle founded the Vanguard Group in 1974 which he still runs. His book is loaded with technical data and charts. It reads easily but should serve better as a reference book for those already familiar with the basics of mutual fund investing.

> Tip: A visit to Barnes and Noble or other good bookstores may be the best way to choose one good reference book which best suits our personal comfort in reading.

Remember to start college or retirement planning as soon as possible. Grampa knows people who begin a program for college before their kids are born. It is worth repeating:

Eric and I love the apple juice at our favorite book store.

> *The advantages*
> *of compound interest*
> *increase almost geometrically*
> *with additional time*.

Let's look again at the chart in Chapter 2 showing the effect of the daily doubling of a penny given on the first of the month. With over half a month gone, on October 16, the

The more time we have for investing, the lower is the re-quired rate of return and the lower the risk we need to take. Just watch our dollars grow, the slower the better!

fund is only $327 but as the days go by, the magic slowly starts to show. On October 20, the sum is $5234. In 10 more days, on October 30, the fund has jumped to more than $5.6 million! And, in one more day, on October 31, the penny-doubling has reached the amazing sum of $10,333,034! Need we say more? Each day, week, month and year adds immeasurably to the growth of our funds. And, also let's not forget: the longer the term of investing, the lower the required rate of return and, of course, the lower the risk we need to take.

Tip: We should consider starting our investing programs yesterday!

Saving programs are essential to good investment planning. The self-discipline needed to save usually runs a distant second to the desire for instant gratification. Spending habits are easy to develop and even harder to curb. The discipline for saving is one that must be taught. In order to establish custom-fitted investment programs, we must accumulate savings. Grampa likes to say:

**"A dollar saved is worth
more than a dollar earned
(after taxes)."**

The subject of budgeting is discussed in many books on financial planning. Charts and forms are readily available without cost from savings banks and life insurance sales people. Forms are found in some computer software which are very reasonably priced such as Intuit's Quicken program.

Tip: Forms are also available from this publisher, Financial Press, in the book *Up Your Equity-Build Your Personal Net Worth.*

Financial Press
P.O. Box 43-2020
Miami, FL 33243

Try the rest first but know, an independent, professional money manager is usually the best choice for investing for college, retirement or whatever the long-term goal is. The advantages are clear.

A good money manager:

- ✔ Takes the necessary time to understand us and our personal needs and goals.

- ✔ Will cut through the maze of individual stocks and mutual funds and make the best choices to fit a portfolio to our personal needs.

- ✔ Makes management and overview of our plans convenient and hassle-free.

- ✔ Serves our needs at surprisingly little expense over the long-term.

- ✔ Is there to guide us through times of panic.

The challenge is to find a qualified money manager who will accept smaller clients. Normally, the minimum investment accepted by most independent managers is in six figures or greater. Since their only compensation is the fees earned based on size of the individual fund, it becomes increasingly more difficult to find a manager who can handle a client in the five-figure range. The usual fee is approximately 1-2.5% of the funds managed depending on the size of the portfolio.

Let's take an example of managing a portfolio of $100,000 with an assumed annual fee of one percent and the arithmetic over the six-year period 1987-1993. This was an exemplary period where even the index funds managed a return in excess of 18% per annum. Let's assume further the money manager performed identically to the 18% average of the Standard and Poor's Index of 500 stocks. The fund in the example thus netted 17% (i.e., 18% minus one percent fee). After all expenses, the $100,000 invested in 1987 grew to $261,120 in 1993. This is more than a 250% return over the six year period. Not bad!

Again, the problem is to find a qualified independent money manager. Some of the major mutual fund companies are beginning to reshuffle their operations to include more no-load funds and are creating advisory and money management services. This creates even more of a maze, increasing the difficulties for the small investor.

Ask the family lawyer or CPA to recommend an independent money manager who accepts smaller clients.

Tip: Ask the family, lawyer, CPA or qualified fee-for-service financial planner to recommend one or two qualified independent, money managers. In South Florida, I am pleased to recommend my dad and his company. Is he an independent and a qualified professional? You bet!

Am I (and his niece Elizabeth) qualified as independent sources? Not really. My dad has already made arrangements to back up Grampa to pay the costs of whatever universities his kids (of course, including me) choose.

Unpredictable events do frequently take the best laid plans of mice, men, grandkids and their families off course. This is where reliable insurance counselling and planning becomes vital. Our parents should prepare, early on in the family planning program, for adequate life, accident and disability insurance coverage. There are some good reference books on the subject of insurance coverage. It is a subject not covered in this book and is an area where qualified financial planners can truly earn their fees.

Tip: To further protect against tapping
into the kids' college savings funds,
establishing separate trusts is recommended. Gift to Minors trusts are
easily created by savings and investment institutions. All mutual funds can
establish such a fund in the initial
application to open the account.

Volatility of a portfolio is what constitutes its measurement of risk. In addition to increased market risk, extreme
volatility also produces restless sleep for
most. For long-term investing strategies,
volatility over a shorter term can be practically disregarded. With an average annual growth of 10.3% of stocks for the past
69 years, it is not worth chasing hot stock
picks. This is especially true when the risk
(volatility) will hardly make a meaningful
increase in the long-term average yield and
even more questionable since an increased
annual return is not even needed! Why
then are stock brokerage and fund companies looking for winners? Grampa says it's
mainly because the intense competition for
customers creates a need for short-term
performance. Brokers and fund managers

Avoid borrowing money from our college funds by obtaining insurance we can afford and setting up our funds under the state's Gift to Minors Act.

turn in their "report cards" every quarter (i.e., three months) for evaluation.

> Tip: Rather than switch to the fund of the year, or reach for higher current yields, measure performance every two or even three years. Switching funds over the shorter term can be risky.

Unless there's a real good reason, we should avoid switching funds every year because of short-term performance reports.

Watch out for confusion generated during market declines by some economists, hucksters and Wall Street consensus opinions. It's always worthwhile considering the contrarian point-of-view which over the longer term may prove to be more valid. When most suggest selling portfolios or funds, Grampa reminds us, *"When we get off the train, more often than not, we get left at the station."*

> Tip: Kids with long-term goals are better off staying fully-invested all of the time.

Xerox, formerly Haloid Xerox Co. came on the scene in the mid 1950s and caught Grampa's eye with its price of $2 per share. An investment of $2000 for one thousand shares 30 years ago would be worth millions today.

How many times have we heard this story? In recent years, it's the story of Walmart. The unanswered question is how many buyers of the initial issue of Xerox managed to stay the course for the long-term? How many more fell to the pressures of short-term cycles with advice to take profits and sell their shares? Grampa doesn't know the actual statistics but he believes it would prove to be only a very small percentage of the original stockholders who stayed the course for the long-term.

It takes special discipline to hold on to winners over the long-term. We should not be tempted to sell because of short-term market considerations.

The average rate of return over the last 10-15 years in the Vanguard Index 500 Fund was 14.5%. This is 50% above the 10% required per our projections!

Tip: An investment in a no-load mutual fund with a good long-term track record is also worth holding for the longer term. This is true for Elizabeth and me who have more than 15 years to go before beginning college. Again, it is especially important to note the May 15, 1994, item in the *New York Times**of the 10 year average annual rate of 14.5% earned by our Vanguard Index 500 Fund particularly since our plan is based on an average required annual compound rate of 10%.

Yearly reviewing of fund performance may be overdoing it. It is usually best to allow for the normal, long-term cycles to develop in accordance with the overall strategy of the fund manager. It is tempting for fund managers to depart from long-term strategies in order to produce better, short-term performance. Nevertheless, it remains a basic truth: short-term strategies are dangerous to our long-term investing health.

Tip: It pays to stick with the long-term managing strategy with a biannual, if not every three- or four-year, review.

* Editors Note: The chart "Five Views of One Fund" on Page 110 was based on information then received from *Morningstar Mutual Funds On Disc*, Morningstar Inc., Chicago, Illinois. Not included in the chart was the 15-year average for Vanguard Index 500 which was calculated at the slightly higher annual average rate of 14.57%.

Zero coupon bonds can be an excellent vehicle to arrange for the semiannual payments of college costs. Separate short-term zero bonds, Treasury notes and even CDs can be purchased to coincide with actual payment dates, even two to five years before each semester's college costs need to be ready.

Simply, this lessens the problem of withdrawal of funds in a time of depressed markets. For example, let's suppose first semester registration is in June 2008. To have the funds ready for this and continuing semiannual payments through 2011, a plan is initiated, let's say, in 2005 to make individual distributions from the stock funds, depending on more favorable market conditions. Purchases will be made of zero-coupon bonds, Treasury notes or even CDs due on June 2008, January 2009, June 2009 and for each semiannual date until 2011, in time for payment of the last semester and graduation.

> Tip: The CollegeSure CD program offers a ready-made plan for guaranteeing the orderly payments of costs as they become due. (See Chapter 8, "College Planning.")

Begin transferring portions of stock funds to zero-bonds, CDs and Treasury notes 2-5 years before college costs are due.

Hopefully, the deliberate repeating by Elizabeth and me of the benefits of disciplined, long-term planning and need for qualified, independent professional help will be heeded as we adopt successful plans for college. At times, we have broken the rules for positive thinking and dwelt more on the negative aspects. An awareness of the pitfalls can be a positive and required first step in the investment planning process.

Elizabeth and I have noted increased media reporting on scams targeting the naive and uninformed investor. *The Wall Street Journal* presented a feature story on July 14, 1994, entitled:

"Investment Talk Shows Become Forums for Dubious Deals, Scams"

There are times when positive planning first requires the elimination of the negatives.

The article's warnings were directed to radio's investment talk-show rip-offs, but are clearly appropriate to scams of all formats. Some of the warnings and advice can be summarized as follows:

→ Beware of infomercials in disguise. These programs are paid for by promoters. When in doubt, call the station.

→ When an investment is being discussed with interruptions offering hotline, and toll-free telephone numbers, call the station.

→ If the investment sounds good but the promoter offers to pick up your check personally or by express service, beware. Scam artists do this to avoid mail fraud.

→ Remember to check out questionable advisors by calling the disciplinary hotline run by the National Association of Security Dealers (NASD) at 800-289-9999.

watch out for rip-offs:

•
radio infomercials

•
payment requested by private express service

•
programs making individual selling appointments

call the NASD at 800-289-999 to check disciplinary actions on advisors.

In Dade County Florida, the school board has tightened its rules. Brokers and financial professionals must disclose annually if any claims or lawsuits have been made against them and each student is given notice that an instructor is not allowed to use his position for personal gain.

On July 22,1994, the *Wall Street Journal* featured an article:

**"Caution Is a Key Lesson
for Investing Classes"**

This time the focus was on fraud in the investment evening classes at high schools and colleges. The article dealt with *"potential conflicts of interest (which) are common when classes are taught by brokers, financial planners and insurance agents who make their living from the commissions on the products they sell."* There have been a large number of settlements made by Prudential Securities to such students in a 1991 lawsuit filed in a Miami, Florida Circuit Court. These students alleged their instructor, a Prudential broker, sold them risky investments after convincing them in class that the investments were safer than CDs.

There are better choices for investment courses. The NAIC (National Association of Investors Corporation) 810-583-NAIC provides low cost membership and offers educational materials, basic courses and excellent computerized programs for investment analyses.

On September 14, 1994, the S.E.C. announced plans for surprise "sweeps" of small and midsize U.S. stock brokerage firms to root out problem stockbrokers.

Our purpose is not to frighten but rather to enlighten. An awareness of the obstacles along the investing highways should make our financial journey safer and more rewarding. Redundancy and repetition, ad nauseam, has been the intended rule rather than the exception. We believe the positives of our story have outweighed the family banter and leg-pulling as well as the above negatives. Hopefully, we all will be able to accomplish what Johnny Mercer proposed in his World War II lyrics:

If you know where you are going, a good road map will help you get there.

"You have to accentuate the positive
Eliminate the negative
Latch on to the affirmative
Don't mess with Mr. In-Between."

Good luck, kids. See you in college!

EDITOR'S NOTE:

On August 19, 1994, Elizabeth's twin brothers, Matthew Gordon and John Joseph, were born. Each will receive, with our compliments, a copy of this book. Individual custodial accounts, under the Florida Uniform Gifts to Minors Act, have been established by Grampa in Vanguard Funds).

Glossary

advisor - an independent professional who performs services for a fee

aggressive growth fund - a high risk fund that seeks maximum capital appreciation

annuity - a program for fixed payments for specified periods usually sold by insurance companies. This is not a suitable vehicle for our long-term planning

balanced fund - invests in both stocks and bonds

capital gains - profit made on sale of securities or other assets which are usually taxed at a lower rate

derivatives - a recent addition to the world of speculative investments where two parties bet on the performance of some agreed benchmark such as options or futures. This is not a suitable vehicle for our long-term planning. Mutual funds which have heavy exposure should be eliminated from our consideration.

diversification - including at least twelve stocks to a portfolio to minimize market risk

growth fund - a fund that invests in well-established companies for long-term growth

growth and income fund - invests for capital appreciation and income (see **balanced fund**)

income fund - invests in stocks paying high dividends

index fund - a fund which represents a portion or all of the stocks in the marketplace

load - sales charge that ranges from 2% to 8.5%

money market fund - invests in short-term money market instruments such as Treasury bills

no-load mutual fund - a fund without direct sales charges

prospectus - the document, usually prepared by lawyers, requiring investors to read contents before investing. It contains information on mutual fund objectives, fees, risks and management

risk factors include:
- market,
- inflation
- bad judgment
- economic

12b-1 fees - marketing fees, ranging from .25% to 1% annually; sometimes called the hidden loads in no-load funds

volatility - the up and down activity in the market; it is a principal measurement of risk

Index